Growth Beyond Death:
Transition Journeys

Beverly Hafemeister
with contributions by Kym McBride

SE Imprints
Cincinnati, Ohio

Growth Beyond Death: Transition Journeys
By Beverly Hafemeister
with contributions by Kym McBride

Copyright: © 2019 by Kym McBride

First Edition All rights reserved

No part of this book may be used or reproduced in any manner whatsoever, including Internet usage, without written permission from the publisher, SE Imprints. In the case of brief quotations embodied in articles and reviews, approval is granted as long as credits are listed. All information is based on the memories and experience of the author. To protect the identity of clients, family, and friends (dead or alive), the authors have changed some of the names of individuals and some identifying characteristics, details, and situations. Although every precaution has been taken to verify the accuracy of the information contained herein, the author and publisher assume no responsibility for any errors or omissions. No liability is assumed for damages that may result from the use of information contained within.

Cover Design by: Beverly Hafemeister
Cover image: Garik Barseghyan, pixabay.com
Edited and formatted by: Ron Frazer

ISBN (print): 978-1-947553-03-3
ISBN (eBook): 978-1-947553-04-0
Library of Congress Control Number:2019910032

Publisher:
SE Imprints, Cincinnati, Ohio
SEImprints.com
SEImprints@gmail.com

Publisher's Cataloging-In-Publication Data
(Prepared by The Donohue Group, Inc.)

Names: Hafemeister, Beverly, author. | McBride, Kym, author.
Title: Growth beyond death : transition journeys / Beverly Hafemeister, with contributions by Kym McBride.
Description: First edition. | Cincinnati, Ohio : SE Imprints, [2019]
Identifiers: ISBN 9781947553033 (print) | ISBN 9781947553040 (ebook)
Subjects: LCSH: Hafemeister, Beverly. | Future life. | Spiritualism. | Death. | Telepathy. | Bereavement.
Classification: LCC BF1311.F8 H34 2019 (print) | LCC BF1311.F8 (ebook) | DDC 133.9013--dc23

Printed in the U.S.A.

Dedication

This book is dedicated to my lovely sister Elaine
whose life is forever with me. Her youthful, dancing girl
photograph holds a special place in my heart, as it will yours,
now that she has transitioned.

Soul Evolution: the Invisible Structure is the partnership company of Beverly Hafemeister and Kym McBride. In this collaboration, they write books together that educate, enlighten and open a conversation with their readership on varied topics of the evolution of the soul.

Their body of work should be seen as a stepping stone to redefine long-held beliefs on a myriad of topics that limits our awareness of the invisible structure, which is in place so that all souls progress through to enlightenment.

Through their trademark interview style, their work opens a two-way street to a team of instructors (in spirit) who teach higher concepts of the ways this invisible structure is formed to lead all souls back to Source. These are not religious constructs, but spiritual. For some, these spiritual concepts have a tendency to bump-up against many religiously taught dogma.

* * *

Contributing to this book was medium Kym McBride,
co-author with Beverly on the
We Got It All Wrong series
For more info: KymMcBride.com

Authors' Publications List

Books by HAFEMEISTER:

Growth Beyond Death: Transition Journeys (e-book)

Books by HAFEMEISTER AND MCBRIDE:

We Got It All Wrong Series:
We Got It All Wrong:
death and grief, heaven and hell, and mental illness
(Book 1), 2017 (print and ebook)

We Got It All Wrong:
prayer, ghosts, spirit guides and the death of children
(Book 2), 2018 (Print and ebook)

Workbooks:

We Got It All Wrong: Companion Workbook for Book 1
Meditative Coloring Book
2017 (print and interactive e-book)

Journals:

Writer's Coloring Journal: A Handcrafted Visual Art
Collection
for Exploration of Colors and Written Words
2017 (print)

See SoulEvolutionSeries.com

Table of Contents

Dedication i
Authors' Publications List iii
Table of Contents v
Prologue. 1
Part 1   Nancy 5
Part 2   Joshua. 21
Part 3   Marvin 37
                Chapter 1. 39
                Chapter 2. 59
                Chapter 3 79
Part 4   Elaine. 99
                Chapter 1 101
                Chapter 2 103
                Chapter 3 117
                Chapter 4 133
                Chapter 5 149
Part 5   Larry 163
                Chapter 1 165
                Chapter 2 181
                Chapter 3 193
Epilogue. 207
Author Biography 222
Glossary. 225
Chart of Intertwined Souls 229

Prologue

On a clear, bright, glorious Saturday with gentle breezes blowing, twenty people assembled for our annual Road Scholar picnic in the little park's pavilion. I sat down at a table where I recognized four long-time board members: Rita, Joyce, Mildred, and Norm. I had worked with these folks for many years, having periodically been on the board from the club's earliest days. An additional person at the table was an unknown woman who was vividly describing her vacation days at an African wildlife refuge for endangered animals. As we chatted, I felt my mind drift away from the conversation. Drifting first to Joyce, I mentally thanked her for being such a dedicated secretary and loyal supporter of our Road Scholar club.

My thoughts then turned to Norm—grateful for the sweet man who served as President and program chairman with such energy and enthusiasm. Next, I fondly recalled the memory of his deceased wife, Donna, who served as his calm, efficient personal assistant, making certain all items Norm organized were properly vetted and proofread for accuracy. I admired how they forged a loving, marital team with each knowing the other's strengths and weaknesses yet quietly willing to give support as needed.

Avid sightseers in their retirement, this couple stepped up their pace of traveling together, often to far and obscure places. I wondered how hard it was for Norm since Donna had died about three years ago after what seemed like a short illness. Today he announced to our table that next week he was going alone to Cuba to visit a friend. I marveled at how Norm was *really* coping with the loss of his wife and traveling companion by forging on with his life.

As I lingered on those thoughts, gradually I had the sense that Donna was here standing behind Norm and me as we sat at one end of the picnic table. But, of course, Donna would be here. After all, these were her friends, too, at this annual picnic.

Therefore, I began talking telepathically directly to her in my head, "I always thought Norm was a nice guy; and I admired the marriage you formed." Donna was pleased and responded that Norm thought kindly of me, too.

"How have you been, Donna? What have you been doing?"

"I've been busy doing things I enjoy. But, it took me a while to get adjusted over here. It wasn't what I expected. No one ever told me before what your now-published book one, *We Got It All Wrong*, taught me. Your book is rather well known here."

I blushed a little because I had heard such comments before from people on the other side. Knowing that our printed words had helped educate others, not only the living but also the dead who were not aware of such non-traditional views, tickled me greatly.

In a flash I thought back to Donna's funeral service and remembered that the people and clergy were mainstream, traditional Christians—nothing extreme in any manner. But obviously Donna, like most people, didn't have a clue as to what life after this Earth one would be like.

The conversations at the picnic grew in size and volume as folks shared their travel adventures with each other in small groups. Hearing Donna in my head became increasingly difficult, so I reluctantly had to say goodbye. I invited her to visit me anytime she wanted, then disconnected. My! What a swell surprise!

Norm was in charge of the picnic program, a lighthearted, audience-participation presentation that itemized ways older people could find fun. At the conclusion of Norm's talk, twice-widowed Mildred, muttered under her breath to me about "Poor Norm now that Donna is gone ... What has he got?"

Wait a minute! He still has Donna. I wanted to correct Mildred, but I hesitated. *No, Beverly, keep quiet*, I told myself. Mildred is a rigidly religious traditionalist who is not open to entertaining the idea that Donna and I were engaged in direct communication, minutes ago, a few feet away from her. As for Norm going to Cuba alone, I suspect Donna, unseen, will go with him. If not, you can bet she will, at least, be there to help him pack his bags so he remembers everything he needs!

Funny, this morning in my waking hours before going to the picnic, I rolled over in my mind the words my deceased friend, Rev. Herb, spoke—all about the importance of maintaining connections between both sides of the veil. The timing was perfect for the chat this afternoon with Donna as a nice demonstration of continuing friendships using that principle.

Lately my concerns have been about how can I help Earth dwellers get over their self-inflicted myth that our loved ones, once they have left their physical bodies, are dismissed from their natural energetic desires to grow and blossom? This one innocent picnic incident was an impetus that focused my attention on the merits of writing a book that could begin to open our eyes to the paradigm shift that is beginning to take place all around us. In this book we'll learn there is plenty we can do to prepare and flourish in life on the other side!

First, Reader, let me explain how I gathered the information for the book you are holding in your hands. My resources started with my personal journal entries of my life experiences. Paying attention to my own life lessons suggested to me that this subject was a logical theme I was pursuing for my education. If I could benefit, others in a similar position would, too.

Next, I reviewed the many formal readings Kym had

channeled in my presence from her guide, Timingo. To my surprise the subject of what transpires on the other side had not been touched. So, I moved on to inquire about the topic with my own spirit guide, Samuel. He was receptive to my stretching my curiosity in that direction. I'm glad he did. As time went on, I began to realize I could send out the desire to contact a deceased friend and the friend could respond to my search. Lo and behold, I didn't need to work through a medium; I could exchange ideas directly with dead friends and family. How wonderful!

The only caveat I had yet to learn was that we people are always seeing things through our own veil, our own slant on what we experienced in life. We need to be mentally blank to be a good receiver of other people's thoughts they are sending to us.

I recorded many question and answer sessions and sometimes spontaneous visits for reference. As a wonderful backup I have my friend Kym McBride who is a sharp, clear, gifted medium and a treasured consultant who doesn't miss a trick. Also, she has a detailed ability to see and describe those on the other side, a talent I do not possess for I do not see, but only hear.

For the reader's convenience, in the back of the book is a glossary of my jargon you might find helpful. I place it there so you won't feel like I'm talking in an esoteric code. Far from the truth! I encourage you to get a copy of Book One and Book Two of the *We Got It All Wrong* series Kym and I wrote. Read it so you will have a fuller understanding of some of these concepts and the earlier stages Kym and I went through to get here. Guides slip us new knowledge all the time as we learn through living. Take your time reading and reflecting on the experiences of the five main characters in this book. Notice how they represent various situations common to everyday people.

❋ ❋ ❋

The first person you will meet is Nancy, a retired nurse who I got to meet and admire since we attended an informal weekly book discussion group where folks enjoyed exchanging spiritual concepts.

Part 1 Nancy

2012 President of Church Board
Solo Vocalist
Energy Healer
Nurse of Multiple Specialties

Nancy  Part 1

February 1, 2015

At 3 am I was sitting in bed, transcribing an old session when I heard telepathically from my friend Nancy, a former nurse, who was at that moment gravely ill in a skilled nursing care facility. Immediately her voice came through to me, saying she wanted to go and was preparing for her transition to the other side.

Days earlier, Nancy's daughter Becky had notified many distant friends of her grave illness, so many took the opportunity to visit Nancy so they could say their farewells in person. Most importantly, her former husband and stepchildren had traveled great distances to visit her in the hospital and mend old wounds. Often Nancy would doze off, but they patiently waited for her to awaken so their healing talks could resume. Happily, closure came to them thanks to Nancy's generous heart, filled with forgiveness and humor.

Today, during Nancy's early morning visit, it was my turn for an audience. Nancy sought me out telepathically to share her deepest feelings about the future. She said she was bone tired. To help I decided to send the best energy I could to Nancy. I asked to be surrounded by higher guides, but was told, probably by my spirit guide Samuel, healing for Nancy was beyond my current skillset. *Too little, too late*, was the verdict. I decided to do it anyway—better to try. Nancy knew she was beyond physical healing; anyway at this stage, she wanted to go. I hadn't known Nancy long, but from our first meeting, we had clicked together easily. I felt she and I were replaying some old healing event from a past life. So, Nancy and I thanked each other for our telepathic chat, then I rolled over to catch a few more Zs before dawn.

February 4, 2015

This afternoon, I visited Nancy in a small, comfortable nursing center. She said she was on 24/7 morphine, which was taking away her brain with hallucinations. She held my hand tightly while I updated her about our book discussion group. I offered to come back tomorrow to read from the book we were currently discussing. The idea brightened her up because she loved exploring probing questions and swapping theories between friends.

The next afternoon I returned, but she was not able to engage in exchanging ideas that sprang from the text. She could no longer participate in her favorite activity. She had said it had been a rough day, so I knew that was my cue to go home. As I left the room, I turned and waved goodbye to Nancy who smiled back at me. I felt I would not see Nancy again, but I didn't realize she would be gone in a few short hours.

In the hallway, her daughter Becky said she was preparing an email asking friends not to visit anymore. "Mom can no longer play the role of gracious hostess or empathetic counselor. For her own good, we have to protect her." However, I was one of the few who the family, acting in response to Nancy's request, allowed to continue to have short visits.

I understood the family's request because it threw me back in time to when my dying father was visited at home by the church's assistant minister. Come to think of it, we requested the assistant because the head minister had what Dad called a "tin" ear; i.e., deaf to other points of view. Dad's broadminded view was what I loved.

For their privacy I left them alone—too long. I should not have dropped my protective vigil. The man drained the last drop of energy from my dad who was seeing himself in the role of gregarious host to this visitor in his household. Dad was exhausted.

The next day, my angry sister phoned the assistant minister to bawl him out for staying so long and not being sensitive to dad's signs of fatigue. She was right. Part of his job description and training should have been sensitivity to the needs of the gravely ill. And, I, as caretaker, learned a painful lesson about being more alert to what was really happening.

February 9, 2015

At 9 a.m. today, I checked my email for the first time since February 5th to discover Nancy had died *that* night after I left her. I cried at her departure and the loss of my friend. Next, I immediately berated myself for being inattentive to her plight over that weekend. Shame on me for not making her a priority. I heaped all the typical blame on myself that we humans tend to do when we are not proud of our behavior.

My next, powerful thoughts jumped to wondering how was she doing? Was she okay? Could I help her? To my astonishment, she answered!

She said she was resting and surrounded by love. She knew she had died. She informed me she hadn't opened her eyes yet, because it felt *so* good to rest quietly for a bit. She had not looked to see where she was.

I said, "Fine, no hurry."

As usual, I doubted myself; I wondered if what I believed I heard was actually true. Samuel verified through Kym that I, indeed, had directly communicated with[1] Nancy.

As requested by Samuel, I atypically went back to bed in the late morning and slept until 6:00 pm. That evening after my long nap, I sewed draperies until 10:30 pm then went back up the stairs to my bedroom, wondering why I felt sad. I knew part of it was about Nancy, but something else was looming.

---

1 See *We Got It All Wrong: Prayer, Ghosts, and the Death of Children* by Hafemeister & McBride. Book 2, Chapter 12, page 262

I heard a voice in my head say, "Because this is the end of your life as you've known it. Tomorrow you will come downstairs to begin a new life." I sat down on the edge of my bed to ponder its meaning. Was today the end of my historic drapery business or the day I got my own book assignment?

My suspicion that turned into knowing is that during that afternoon nap, I had attended a previously scheduled meeting with my guides and Nancy. They explained to me that it was now time to begin working on the transition book that I had promised in my outline to write during this life. Nancy was to be my first personal introduction to the topic, my first case study. Indeed, today was a serious monumental shift in my whole life's direction.

February 9, 2015

Reading for Beverly Hafemeister channeled by Kym McBride:

Beverly (B), Kym (K), Samuel (S)

B: Samuel, since learning from Becky's email that her mom Nancy died Thursday evening, I'm hearing multiple voices. I think I've identified you and Nancy, but I'm hearing people I can't recognize. Also I've been feeling compassion pouring over me. Can you help me understand?

S: First, the input of compassion was from me offering my condolences.

K: I feel him softly stroking your hand. Meanwhile in the distance, I see Nancy skipping like a young child.

S: There is joy in the amazing feeling of no longer being tied down. Imagine how different it is when you feel your body has let you down for a long time but suddenly the tethers are gone. Realize that young Nancy is on a joyous journey to be free of attachment to her body.

B: Yes, I witnessed Nancy's physical struggles and am glad they are over. But I didn't realize she would be gone a few hours after I visited her. Since then, I'm aware I've talked to Nancy and you. Does that mean others are talking to me, too?

S: All these other voices you hear are *your* fears—your fear bubbles around death are popping up.

B: What's this phenomenon—connected to my fears—you're describing as bubbles, Samuel?

S: The moment you read the email you emotionally connected to the loss of Nancy and made a path that the belief bubbles from your past lives could travel. Beverly, these fear bubbles are coming from your different past lives with their different personalities, reflecting their different ways of grieving in those past lives. Your loss today is hitting something all those bubbles can now relate to—grief.

The bubbles from the past are just popping to the surface and dissipating, pop and dissipate, pop and dissipate. Let them dissipate. Don't hold on to them! You are providing a way for those old beliefs to move up and be released from previous lives, previous sadness, and how your other lives dealt or didn't deal with their grief. They are pockets of unfinished healing. Don't interpret them, just let the bubbles come to the surface and pop. This is a healing process for previous negativity.

Any negative grieving statements you heard were not against you as Beverly. It was grief and anger expressed from your past lives. As a logical being, you filled in the blanks, assuming the words were personally directed at you. Don't listen! This process is not meant for reasoning. Just let them pop and go.

You're currently in grief. It's going to take a process for you to deal with this particular Beverly life grief—that of losing a dear friend. Whatever words or feelings are said or felt, just let them pass through. Don't even worry about what you're hearing. Just let it go. Don't believe anything—even if they're your own thoughts. Let it go. Grief's not always logical.

You're emotionally releasing tons of unfinished, unhealed grief and loss from previous lives and some parts of this life. None of it needs to be thought about; just feel and release; feel and release. You're working on your current grief; and it's a good thing because you have made a pathway for healing past life grief, too.

B: Yes, I like your calm approach in healing. When talking with Nancy, she knew she was out of her physical body, surrounded by love, and enjoying the peaceful quiet. I nervously asked her where she was; what she saw. She was so content she hadn't bothered to open her eyes!

As her friend, I was hoping that she did not feel alone or stuck somewhere. I wanted to help her have a smooth transition into the next phase of her journey if she was in need.

S: If we can be honest here, you also figured, "She'll never be a part of any of our books as a sounding board for me as well as a personal loss."

B: [*smiling*] Yes, you don't miss a trick. But, I was also a bit disappointed her message to me was not a detailed travel log. I wanted to know where she was, what she was experiencing, and how she was feeling. Now that Nancy has died, my thoughts moved to, "Can we continue our relationship? Or, must our paths separate?" Was she just in my life as a "sweet treat" relationship, but that was now over?

Because I quickly felt so close to Nancy once we met, do I assume correctly we've been associated before?

S: Yes, definitely.

B: Like me, she is a *Warrior*[2] who rescues spirits who have imprisoned themselves?

S: No, but she's a companion member of the deliverance team. You are side by side—different, but closely related to the warrior *soul cluster* group. Warriors are taking spirits out of their hell illusion, but they don't necessarily see what happens to these traumatized spirits afterward. Nancy's group, as a companion, comes in to soothe that soul who just went through the dramatic experience of living in hell.

B: In other words, she travels along with the warriors. After we release people, she's there with her group?

---

2   See glossary and *We Got It All Wrong*, Book One and Book Two for explanations of Warriors, Soothers, Rejuvenators and Soul Clusters.

K: Let me explain to you what Samuel was showing me. Nancy is a *Soother*, not a warrior, but she does work at the soul's next stage. I saw you standing next to each other. I felt you were in one group while she was in another group, but closely connected.

Also, I felt this huge "ahh" like a release coming from a soul just rescued. As a visualization of her job description, I saw Nancy come in, wet down their brow with a towel offering comfort. This is what the soothers do for souls who are living their trauma over and over again. She does important work to help them get over their original choice to punish themselves. She's happy to be doing this work full time now. Finally, Nancy's able to do what she's always wanted to do without other things distracting her—like Earth life.

When her soother patients are ready, they are handed off to a group we've called *Rejuvenators*. From there the soul begins the process of rehabilitating their lives.

B: Thank you, Kym, for telling me about Nancy and the joy she feels about her new, full-time work. I know her to be a loving, energetic person who will be a great benefit to her group. It's wonderful information about her work.

February 10, 2015

Our book discussion group that had been faithfully attended by Nancy met for the first time since her passing. Today's class included minister Doris, Bill, Suzanne, Judy, and me, Beverly. During our group's silent meditation period, Nancy told me in my head how happy she was and how beautiful everything looked on the other side. Also, she remembered being there before. Stunned, I remained silent.

As the class began, Doris made it a point to invite Nancy out loud to be part of our class. To my surprise our energy increased Nancy's field of vision! In other words, the more energy we sent her, the more powerfully she could connect to the group session, which was new information for me.

Next I heard Nancy ask me to do her a favor, "Thank Doris for all she did for me. I hadn't been able to thank her enough."

Nancy was determined to find a way to contact each of the group members at a later time, but now I was to be the message bearer. I relayed these individual messages as best I could. Bill validated his information because he'd already heard the same message from another source earlier—unknown to me.

One last message for all of us: Nancy advocated that living people keep remembering the "dead," because they continue to want to be in our lives. "Let them know we work tirelessly for the living on the other side and feel good about our help."

February 12, 2015

At Nancy's funeral service at the church, to my surprise, Nancy impressed on me that she could put her arms around everyone and hug them. This description is not a figure of speech she insists. (I can't understand, but I will take her word for it.)

After Nancy's funeral, Bill came up to me, hugged me, and profoundly thanked me for speaking up at our book discussion group to tell them about my experiences with Nancy, her response in the care center, and her early transition phase before opening her eyes as we meditated. So Bill, who knew me to be a shy person reticent to speak, helped me make a mental shift finally to see and accept what I have been given as a gift to be shared.

More clarity came to me when I asked my guide again why I was sad going upstairs to bed. He reiterated, "You're going up as one person, but tomorrow you'll come down as another person. The gift is to help grieving people bridge the transition periods in their life."

The book you are now reading is one result of that change in my life direction.

Here's a summary of my journey in which I started to hear voices beyond the normal self-talk we all experience:

Three or four decades ago, I read a book (title and author forgotten) with individual chapters describing such gifts as speaking in tongues, interpreting tongues, clairvoyance, etc. Additionally, clairaudience is one of these gifts. Now I believe that is a gift I had when I arrived in this life, but I was not to open it until late in life. This happened. Latent talent opened the door. However, I did not become aware of several things about this ability. I did not know that I could also receive and hear words from:

- My spirit guides
- My deceased family and friends
- Troubled aspects of previous lives that I avoided until I had the skills to remove them
- Voices from my warrior activities and travels
- Imprinted, residual, traumatic conversations of other people
- And other voices of yet unknown sources

I questioned my mental stability when these voices appeared:

- My current, highly sensitive persona is nicknamed "Tender Beverly" by the other side.
- My inability to comprehend clues and straight talk given to me by the other side
- My inability, yet need, to discern the source of most voices
- Not realizing clairaudience is a gift to help myself and others, not a detriment.
- My judgmental desire to separate messages as good or bad. Do not downplay its importance. How many suicides have happened to those who didn't evaluate who was speaking?

March 21, 2015

While I was in my studio, sewing drapery panels for a museum, and while Kym was busy sorting out her files, I, without intention, made a connection with Nancy. I began by summarizing Nancy's words but quickly moved to write the exact words as spoken to me.

Nancy sounded good. She said she's now slowly reviewing this recent life. A person is allowed to do that as slowly as they desire. She said she was pleased and surprised to feel she had done better than she realized she had.

(I chuckled and declared, "Are you crazy! Well, of course!" because I and others had long recognized the goodness in her. Why are we so tough on ourselves?)

Nancy said all this review is done lovingly with great care and empathy for what the soul has just experienced. *Don't worry!* She cautioned. It's not hurtful or painful. It's just a matter of knowing what and why you did what you did. Very comforting! She said she worried too much about always getting everything right.

Nancy told me, "You, Beverly, have the same problem of always wanting to make wise decisions. Don't worry. It's all fine. Just make your decisions and follow that path until you reach the conclusion. If you don't like the outcome, then backtrack and pick up another thread. Redo on this Earth if you can or want to. Try another approach and see where it takes you and whether you like it better.

"I just wanted to touch bases with you as you sit and sew. Say 'Hi' to everyone. Keep me in your prayers. You have no idea how important that is and how helpful prayer is to us on the other side no matter how long we've been over here. Keep in touch with all your loved ones and all your "enemies." Put that in quotes because we have no enemies. They are all just souls playing roles in our lives.

"Kym is right in the main, but you need to be more assertive about her language and her attitude that is not in alignment with yours. (She likes to cuss; and you figure she attracts negative energy.) You're being too helpful so that now you are becoming an enabler to the very traits she's trying to get rid of. I love her and see what a great blessing she is to you and others, but she's also there to help you confront your weak tendencies. It is a blessing from God that you are together now. Make the most of it. Nothing lasts forever. This, too, will change.

"I've never seen you at night in your warrior work, but I feel your energy and know you are helping others. During the daytime, you could do more at the Tuesday discussions. These folks need your broader insight. We all need new perspectives to consider choices. You offer something more that they can hear and process as they wish. Life is always full of choices—the more the merrier!

"I've been amazed where I currently am—how much the souls here love to discuss various theories, my favorite past time. So, get ready! On the other side, at least for people like us, we are still enjoying the give and take of conversations, theories, etc.

"Love to all! I see you've reached the end of your notepaper. My best regards to Kym. I think she's super; yet, like all of us, a diamond in the rough. Just help her smooth out the edges!

"Love you!"

P.S. After typing up my notes, I asked the universe if there was anything more to add. I was told Nancy had left, but it was her hope I would convey the information to the people at our book discussion group. I did.

March 29, 2015, Palm Sunday

I wanted to go by the post office to drop off some letters, so I took I-71 to church in Kentucky on the same route Nancy routinely used. Not surprisingly, I sensed her in my car's passenger seat. She announced herself by saying she enjoyed seeing the route again. When we got to the Kennedy exit, she reminisced, "This is the exit I always took to go to Becky's house. I did it so many times, I could practically drive it blindfolded."

As we approached the vicinity of the church, I stopped my car to pull out the portable road signs from my trunk advertising the presence of our new congregation on the Kentucky side of the Ohio River. It was important people knew we were there.

When we got to church, Nancy said, "Thanks for the lift. Don't wait up for me; I'll find my way back when I'm ready. I'll not get in your way; I just wanted to attend church early to help set up the greeter's table."

Indeed, in life Nancy loved welcoming visitors and helping them feel comfortable. It was her joy; and we loved her cheerful dedication.

As she got out of my car, I inquired of Nancy, "Who did you bring to church with you? Anybody?"

"Nobody. Never thought of that!"

I could tell it was a new idea in her mind; and she would give it some thought by next Sunday.

I joked, "We gotta work both sides of this river and this world." I figured there were many church attendees I never saw in a body. Certainly, Nancy was one that Sunday. I'm assuming their prayer energy is just as beneficial to all of us.

April 7, 2015

Discussion group check-in comments about Nancy's impact on our Easter Sunday service:

- Doris said she had been nudged by Nancy to do the flower ceremony and other inspired ideas for the service.
- According to Becky, Nancy manned the entrance welcome table where she felt most comfortable.
- Bill said she waved to him during the meditation phase of the service.
- Bev told about Nancy hitching a ride to church on Palm Sunday.
- Suzanne said Nancy told her to get her will in order and prepay funeral expenses for harmony later.

Wasn't it nice that we as a group could so freely talk about contacts with our beloved friend from the other side? If more friends and families could frankly talk like this, I wonder if grief could be less painful?

November 29, 2015

Nancy stopped by for a visit and left these messages:

N: Bev, I loved our time together, miss it, but it's the same when you are here. We love it here, but we always choose not to stay long. I regret to tell you that, Beverly, because you want a rest, but I'll bet you'll be back to Earth as soon as you see it's needs. So, do what you can now to make Earth a better place to receive you in your next life. Not a threat, just a reality check. [*smile*]

You can go anywhere and will probably choose many places at once, like you and I are now doing. Yes, this is verification of your work. I can't give you details because only our guides know it all. They don't want to overwhelm you. They are unbelievably lovely and loving.

Please tell people alive on Earth to get their act together, and stop expecting us on the other side to heal their wounds. Earth life is where you do that, not here. Here you're just planning your next life to remove things you came there earlier to do. Stop kicking the can down the road. Hate to use a cliché, but it's understood.

B: What are your needs, Nancy?

N: Pray for me. Remember me to others and ask for them to send their prayers, too.

B: Do I work with you?

N: Actually, it's our other soul fragments that are more intensely connected in this life than you and I are. We just got the overflow of their friendship.

OBSERVATIONS LEARNED FROM NANCY:

- Just by thinking of deceased persons brings them forth.
- Five days before dying Nancy had decided to leave and was preparing for transition.
- Leaving a disabled, physical body is a joyous relief for the deceased.

- Fear bubbles of grief and anger from the mourner are to heal past grief. Let the bubbles pass without listening to them. Feel and release. An escape path is being created for removal.
- Our life review after death can be done at as slow a pace as the deceased desires. Review is lovingly done with great empathy.
- We have no enemies—just souls playing various roles in our lives.

Nancy had the luxury of waking up at her own leisurely pace because she felt comfortable that she was in a safe place. In the next section, you will meet a bewildered man who had a totally different experience when crossing over to the other side. As it happened, I, though distracted by my own night work concerns, was able to help reorient him when lost and desperate for assistance.

Part 2 Joshua

Student Conservation Volunteer, 1992
Sugarbowl Ski Resort Worker, Lake Tahoe
Whitewater Rafting Guide, Tennessee
U.S. Air Force Firefighter

Joshua  Part 2

July 21, 2015

At our local, book discussion group, I was greatly saddened in disbelief to learn that Josh, our friend Suzanne's son, died two days earlier. Unfortunately, Suzanne had been out of touch for a fortnight of kayaking near Savannah, so she knew nothing about her youngest son being in critical distress for nine days. Apparently Josh called emergency when he continued feeling sick and was admitted to the hospital, but after seven days in the hospital his body continued to deteriorate and progressively shut down.

Even though this turn of events was frightening and tragic, it was not the first time mother and son had experienced wrenching life adjustments. Perhaps occasional injuries were to be expected with an adventurous, courageous son like Josh. After all, he had chosen to be in the U. S. Air Force as a firefighter where part of his training was learning how to parachute safely out of airplanes as a matter of course.

The irony of fate came when, while still a young man, he went hiking after work with his two dogs and a friend. On a lark, Josh climbed up a tree—a very big tree, approximately thirty feet high—lost his balance and fell into a dry creek bed. He knew immediately he was seriously hurt because he could feel blood coming out of his ears. His friend ran to get help, which took about an hour and a half. Since it was dark by then, the rescuers had a hard time locating him. Fortunately, every time they called to him, his two dogs barked; and that's how they were able to find him.

All the ensuing surgeries and recovery periods created bittersweet, bonding times for mother and son. In the end Josh was confined to a wheelchair. Yet, through the journey they shared together in this life, their souls were linked as closely as you would expect to find with soul fragments.

With limited mobility, doing simple tasks in life weighed heavily on this strong, athletic man. Josh struggled with occasional depression. Fortunately, vigorous wheelchair athletics gave Josh a real ego boost. A buddy of his even went so far as to invite him to parachute piggyback on him to brighten his day, but sustaining enthusiasm was a challenge. Living in a wheelchair for the next fifteen years took a mental toll on Josh and wore down his self image as a productive human being.

At the time of his death, he had been living independently with his German shepherd near his divorced mom, yet an enormous mental challenge for Josh was personal forgiveness. I saw how Josh's disability and mental angst created turmoil in an already stressed family when his frustrations overflowed into temper displays. As with any unfinished business, I grieve for his loss and his mother's loss. I didn't know him long, but I always found myself drawn to him.

The day of Josh's memorial service, I had a looming sense of trouble, which I didn't understand. I left my house early, took a wrong turn, twice almost got hit by another car, couldn't find a parking spot, so I left my car across the busy highway just as the military gun salute began to honor this young, air force veteran.

Trying to be inconspicuous in the crowded room, I was able to find the last empty seat in the back row. Finally relaxed enough to settle down in my chair, I heard a voice in my head that identified himself as Josh.

Somehow I had the sense he was airborne, scanning the

audience with his own radar searching for people. I'm ashamed to admit I was hoping not to be spotted. He said he could "see" my light (whatever that means) and recognized me. Maybe that's why I had a hard time driving to the funeral home. Disappointed to be singled out, I said in my head:

Beverly (B), Joshua (J)

B: Are you okay?

J: Yes.

B: Do you know you are dead?

J: Yes. A few days ago I knew that.

B: [*thinking of my experience with Nancy*] Are your eyes open? Can you see anything around you? Do you know where you are?

J: No, I can't see well, but I recognize minister Doris' voice and can begin to make out images when she speaks. Can you do me a favor? Please wait so you are the last to greet my mother. She's really going to need someone.

Lingering as requested, I, Beverly, was one of the last people in line to comfort Suzanne and give her a big hug. But I wasn't the only one to loiter, so I figured Josh had been successful in finding more recruits.

Later I discovered Josh had witnessed a pre-service cloistered meeting between his parents. If Josh could not see but recognized the minister's voice, certainly he could recognize his own father's voice and be drawn to attend that unpleasant confrontation. As a result, his mother had taken quite a verbal beating from the demands made by her former husband before the service started. I was of small help in Josh's efforts to protect his mom at this time of family friction. Not having questioned his exact instructions at the time, I felt badly when I later learned of the angst of Suzanne's former husband before the service began and the helpless position Josh must have felt he was in. Clearly there was a lot more going on with the Josh story than I was aware.

❋ ❋ ❋

B: May I talk to you and our spirit guides, Josh? Samuel told me that I needed to straighten out my unknown parts about how I happened to spot you when lost in space after your death. This is important transition information I need to take off the top shelf and describe now for the record.

J: Yes, I'm willing to give it a try. If at any stage I find it is too difficult to talk through you, I'm going to ask you to please have Kym do this reading. Is that agreeable?

B: Yes, that is in line with my thinking. I would like to have accuracy, so please, if my channeling needs to stop, I want you to pull the plug on this. Then I will ask Kym to step in.

J: Thank you. Just keep your mind as empty as you can. I will speak loudly and slowly so you can get my words. Now then, you are wondering how did you ever see me and rescue me? That is a legitimate question.

After I died in the hospital, I found I was in a dark place. I was frightened and very much alone. I didn't know what to do. I saw you passing by; I assume on your way home. You were headed back to your bedroom, back into your body, to continue on with your sleep for the evening.

I yelled at you, but you didn't look my way. For some reason, I couldn't get your attention. I became extremely upset as I yelled and yelled at you. You simply hurried past me; I couldn't figure out why. Here was somebody who should recognize me but didn't. Alarmed, I began to circle around you to try to catch your eye.

At that time I did not know anything about spiritual job assignments. I didn't know you had night missions, much less know that I was, also, a warrior. Neither did I know I was related to such people. The concept of bands of trained volunteers called warriors who willingly accepted the assignment of rescuing lost souls trapped in self-styled hells was totally alien to me during my Earth life.

I later discovered you were distressed about that evening's

warrior mission. You were wanting to block it and everything else out of your mind because you were upset and wanted to shake it from your memory so you would have no visual image of that particular assignment.

Now I understand. As a warrior myself, I have had many missions of that type. I know how brutal they can be, so there's no need to apologize because I, from personal experience, know how rough it can be. Your missions aren't always that way, but when it is rough it is *really* rough. However, we won't dwell on those tasks here.

Now, I would like to get back to the time when I was circling around you trying to be noticed. Instead of feeling comfortable, I found myself, and believed myself to be, alone in an endless black abyss. I could not easily see.

I know now that I was not alone nor in an endless pit. Instead my anger had built this frightening space. Furthermore, unknown to me, I was surrounded by entities whose assignment it was to keep an eye on me, keep me safe from harm and keep me on course.

Eventually with enough circles, I got your attention; and you saw me with your eyes. You recognized me and magically lowered my barrier so these other entities could reach me and securely take me to where I needed to go. I did not feel it at the time, but I was the one in the dark, blocking them from helping me to the light. To me that's an indication of a loving God.

Some of the sharp readers will think, "Does that make my will stronger than God's?" My Josh answer to that is, "Yes, that's what free will is all about. We have been empowered to overwhelm God's best intentions for us." As you imagine that kind of message is not going to sit very well with the average church-going person. Some will think it is heresy, but it is not. That's my experience—that I was so powerful, resistant and angry with myself that I was keeping help away from me when I so desperately needed assistance.

Beverly, I hadn't read your book until I arrived on the other side. As you know, after I read it, I nagged my mother to read your book. I insisted she could learn and better understand what life is like in the parts we are not consciously aware. I have been grateful for the use of the book and I thank you and Kym for writing it.

Now, the people who read your book will not know if they have your ability, too. They will think that I don't travel at night, I'm not a warrior. I don't see things. What use will this information be to me?

This is my important message to you and the readers of this book. At death a percentage of spirits, like me, will be angry with themselves about how their lives were going and about their slowness to adjust. They are likely to duplicate what I inflicted upon myself. Therefore, when a loved one dies, it's *extremely* important that you pray for their safe arrival on the other side and that there will be no barriers that keep them from the love of God. Those barriers that we people are able to generate are so strong that we can repel God's help. We people have to be our own best friends and allow help to come through us.

Yes, I was annoyed at you at the memorial service because you were trying to hide from me without understanding how much I needed a friend to watch over my mom after the service. In fairness to you, you had no idea about the events that transpired earlier in the morning. That conversation was degrading to my mom's welfare, so I was in a protective mode. For some reason you were not attuned to the seriousness of what I was talking about. I don't hold it against you, but I want you to know my reaction.

I see you want to respond to me but are afraid you can't talk and keep your head empty at the same time. [*chuckles*] That's okay. I know from what you have written that it wasn't a proud moment for you. So, I accept what you say and bear no ill will toward you.

B: Thank you, Josh.

J: In many sections of this book, you're writing in-depth, uncomfortably personal accounts of yourself and your family situations. It's not for me to say what should be divulged, but I see it's a question in your mind at all times. As far as my situation goes, sharing this reading is fine at this stage, so I thank you for visiting with me.

B: It's my pleasure; and thank you for telling me the backstory of your transition, Josh. Goodbye for now.

❄ ❄ ❄

January 23, 2016

Picking up my story where we left off after Josh's memorial service, I sent his mom this email:

> Suzanne,
>
> FYI twice now while Kym and I were editing our second book, Josh announced his presence by chilling Kym. The first time I saw Kym jump with surprise was when she saw him sitting in the chair by our worktable. I don't see spirits, but he spoke to me to say he was jumping for joy that his mom decided to read our first book. He'd been encouraging you to read it and was happy you're getting exposed to some of these concepts.
>
> This morning Kym saw Josh again in the chair. I wasn't privy to the conversation, but I noticed Kym shed a tear. I'm happy a good connection between Kym and Josh is taking place. Was thrilled to hear you are meditating, Suzanne. Good things will happen because you both desire the connection to remain. You Go Girl!
>
> Bev

❄ ❄ ❄

January 25, 2016

Suzanne's Email response to Beverly:

> The thought of you and kym connecting with josh is so exciting! When you say, "you saw him in the chair," did you mean the chair at your house, or his wheelchair? Just curious bc I don't see him in the wheelchair at all. He was immediately released from that the minute he departed this

dimension—at least that's the way I see it. When you say "moved to tears," I'm guessing that means it was a heartfelt, and loving connection. I cry the entire time I'm meditating bc the connection is so strong. Do you think Kym has the time and energy to have a session with me some time in the near future? I've been getting very positive and loving messages from him all along, and would love the opportunity to explore this in more detail.

Talk soon! Love, suzanne

❊ ❊ ❊

February 2, 2016

Today is Groundhog Day, and I, Beverly, am here at home sitting alone upstairs while Kym is downstairs working. A spirit guide has telepathically asked me to channel a message from him. He calls himself Oliver. The message concerns Suzanne and her deceased son, Josh.

B: If the guide Oliver would like to begin, I can hear him easily enough.

O: Thank you, Beverly.

Suzanne and Josh, I want you to know, I've been asked to come together here to let you know we are all connected in a pod of cells known as a soul. We are all segments of the same soul. I can't tell you how many people are in this group, but Beverly knows another person who is in our group. Suzanne, you know Herb as the pseudonym Hal through the book series Beverly and Kym have been writing. I refer to him so that you will have some frame of reference. Where to start?

I want you to know that my name is not Oliver. I go by different names: Samuel for Beverly, Stanley for Herb, and different names for the two of you, Suzanne and Josh. Actually I'm the same fellow. I'm sorry about the confusion, but there seems to be a rule that people not know who they're connected with until they're ready to enter that doorway and meet the other fragments in their group.

I'm kinda the head of this group as your main spirit guide.

I'm happy with that task and want the best for all of you because I love you. I think Beverly has finally caught on that she is loved by me.

Let's address some information about Beverly that will help all of you before I move on to others. I'm not only the foolish prankster I have projected to Beverly, but I have serious messages for her to help improve her life here on Earth. The progress made on Earth greatly increases the progress a soul continues to make on the other side. Thus, I'll help her life on the other side, too, when she arrives, whenever that is.

We're all helping each other as you have read in the published readings from Timingo and me through Kym. At that time Beverly could not hear any kind of voices that were coming to her from us because they were being drowned out by her own problems, her own past lives, and her other problems in this life that needed to be adjusted and cleared away before she could make progress to hear us on her own.

She's now reached the stage where she can hear our voices. She is still in the learning stage of distinguishing which voices come from where but she's catching on. We think soon she will be much better at it; and we're hopeful it will come soon because the inability to sort out the voices hinders her progress.

Let me get to you folks. I want you to know that there is no one who loves you more than your Father in heaven. He asks me to let you know how important it is for you folks to enjoy each other's company on Earth and after. Some of you have already transitioned back to the other side.

Our Heavenly Father wants us to make as much progress as we can on Earth so we can continue to advance forward and to help others move ahead, too. It's extremely important that you keep helping each other.

Suzanne, your son Josh is a person who *was* in a state that's called limbo. Beverly was able to find him out there because in his life, she was very fond of him. She didn't know why, because she hadn't had that much contact with him, but a bond was there. Somehow she recognized him spinning in the air without the ability to steady himself and get oriented. She was the one who helped steady him and move him into a safe place. Beverly has no idea she did this because it's a part of her night work as a warrior. A little bit of that was in Book One, but not a lot. The second book of the *We Got It All Wrong* series described the various jobs people have on the other side. A warrior is one of those people.

As I say, Beverly was able to recognize him, to reach out to him, and take him to the place that Beverly knows when she's asleep but not when she's awake. When she is awake, she is absolutely unaware of all of the stuff going on. She just knows that somehow she has helped somebody because she always wakes up very happy and very much alive. As the day progresses she gets wound down because the life of a warrior is very difficult.

Working with rude, crude, lost and disempowered people in her night work weighs her down, but the joy she gets from helping find somebody and rescuing them brightens her day as she begins the mornings. Now she's becoming more and more aware of these people coming to her during the daytime. Frankly, she's getting exhausted because she's still having difficulty sorting out who's there, what they want, and what she can do about it.

I hope that explains to all of you, what her job is and how it has helped you and helped us as a soul group. So we thank Beverly for her diligence and her ability to spot Joshua when he was in such need.

Now on your part Josh, you were spinning out of control because you were so upset with yourself about having, first, gotten injured, and second, your conduct after being paralyzed and taking it out on your mother. Yet, she was the person who probably loved you the most and cared for you the most during that time. So there is a lot of hurt between the two of you—you hurting yourself, and she feeling like the recipient of your verbal abuse.

As to you, Suzanne, my analysis is that you feel disappointed and let down that you couldn't have helped your son more than you did. You're beating up on yourself and living in the past, trying to replay and rethink, "I should have done this; I should have done that" when really there was nothing you could do. You wore yourself down by putting pressure on yourself and making yourself feel guilty.

It's what we guides find constantly about Earth people. Humans rarely seem to understand that they are hurting themselves as much or more than they are hurting other people. Somehow society has gotten the notion that other people must come first; and we must come last in caregiving, if at all. Actually it's the other way around. It's like the adage they give when you enter a plane, "In case of emergency, you put on your own face mask first and then you reach out to help others." It's the same way in Earth life. You've gotta help yourself first.

I've got all of you assembled here to remind you all that you have that same problem. You haven't been able to let go of the past and take care of yourselves. You're constantly in a state of "I did wrong; I made a mistake; how could I have been so stupid?" All those kind of thoughts beat you down. It's not at all helpful for anyone.

When you're down, everything around you is down. When you have enough of that, you start building your own hell on Earth. I want you to know there is no such thing as hell, but we create our own hell by the images we build around ourselves, the vision we have of ourselves. Constantly, people are putting themselves into hell.

As an example, I'll tell you about a past life of Beverly. In chapter 8 of *We Got It All Wrong*, Book One, there is mention of the sorceress, a person who, in her lifetime, did something she thought was wrong, so she could never forgive herself. She isolated herself and eventually committed suicide because she thought she was so worthless. Because of that, not because of the suicide, but because of her thought pattern of "I'm not good enough," she ended up in a hell situation where she locked herself up in a castle turret, closed the shutters, and stayed in the dark to punish herself.

In this lifetime, Beverly's major mission is to find a way to release this woman who we're nicknaming the sorceress so she could escape the prison that she created for herself. Once that is accomplished, the rest of her soul fragments and her past lives will benefit from what the released sorceress and Beverly learn. Since you are all soul fragments, it affects you personally.

I know this is heavy stuff, but I think you can probably follow what I'm saying easily enough. If not, I'm always here whenever you desire, Beverly, Herb, Suzanne, and Josh.

We also have someone listening in who I have not introduced. That person has the same problem of self-esteem just as the others presented here. Now, they don't happen to be part of our soul group, but as Beverly says, "The other side doesn't waste energy. When there is an opportunity to give a message to somebody, they'll add as many people as possible to listen to the message."

I hope this is a help to you. I appreciate being able to talk to you as a group.

Now that I'm finished, I'm going to go around to each one of you and tingle your legs to let you know I'm here—starting with Beverly.

B: [*Without consciously feeling a physical sensation, Beverly emotionally chuckles then weeps*].

O: And I thank you.

I'll go around to the next person; they can feel what I'm doing. Then I'll go to the last person. Their reaction tells me if they can feel it, too. So I want you to know when you feel that sign, you'll know I'm present. It doesn't matter what I look like. It doesn't matter what I sound like or what my name is; it's my energy you're going to recognize. You'll know who's visiting you.

❄ ❄ ❄

February 6, 2016

Email from Suzanne to Beverly:

> Oh my gosh, Beverly! This is so interesting. It very much saddens me that Josh was spinning out-of-control. I didn't realize that. Any connection I ever had with him—he seemed very calm and peaceful. He came to me the day after he died. He was calm and hugged me, and told me he loved me. Maybe he was still on the earthly plane at that time. Anyway, I'm sooooooo thankful you recognized him and rescued him. Does that mean he's out of limbo now and in a good place? As for the rest of the story, it's very accurate. I always knew Joshua was beating himself up over injuring himself in the first place, and I knew he had great remorse for how his condition affected me. And it's very true that I always felt inadequate in helping him. All I wanted after that was to relieve his suffering somehow. I knew too that his suffering was self-imposed, just like his injury.
>
> I haven't felt the tingling on my leg yet, but I'm sure it will come, and I'll know exactly who it is. Thank you so much for sharing this with me.
>
> I'm planning to go to a special event at the dharma center.
>
> Talk soon. Love you

In the next section of the book you will meet my former husband where we learn we can begin to heal our past missteps now rather than wait until we are both on the other side.

Part 3 Marvin

1955 High School Grad
Boston Marathon Runner
Trumpet Player
Men's Chorus Tenor
Physical Education Teacher
Author's Husband

Marvin  Chapter 1

February 29, 2016

Beverly (B), Kym (K), Marvin (M)

Out of the blue in February I received an official form letter from the Social Security Office asking me to come into their headquarters in April with my official vital statistic paperwork—birth, wedding, and divorce certificates. I wondered, *why would they want to see me?*

Nonetheless, I set about locating my copies of these legal documents. A little uncertain about my divorce papers, I decided in March to swing by for an unofficial stop to double check what I was planning to bring for my official date in April. I didn't want to be caught empty handed with the wrong papers.

In April I returned to discover I was eligible for an increase in my monthly allotment. After I answered a series of questions, the staff member figured up my generous, new monthly benefits. Item by item she efficiently explained the rates. As I was getting ready to departed, my curiosity unabated I asked, "But why?"

"Your former husband has died." I staggered backwards as teardrops welled up in my eyes with that official pronouncement. Eventually, as I stood gazing out the reception room windows to steady myself, I heard a voice in my head and knew it was Marv—but not as I knew him. Religiously speaking, as I knew him, he had always seemed to be a run-of-the-mill, lackluster Christian without much curiosity. Now he spoke as one much more broadly enlightened.

He now understood how in this life, we were both playing roles in each other's lives. I was tickled to hear he had reached that understanding on the other side, but like most of us, didn't have that concept while actually in his physical body. His words and tone were comforting, but I did not have a recorder in my pocket or in my car to capture his words as I drove away. I can only go on memory today.

By the time I reached home, much to my surprise, I had tapped into and needed to vent my long held resentment and anger. His "proof" that he *didn't wish me "any harm"* back then fell flat on my ears. So telepathically I asked, "If you didn't wish me harm, why did you pick the only notoriously garbage-mouthed, underhanded lawyer in our county to represent you in court? Did you know he was so underprepared that my lawyer had to spend time, which, by the way, I had to finance, to bring your lawyer up to speed on the details of our case? Once the divorce judgment was pronounced under the new no-fault rules, I had to pester your lawyer to let me know what cash I was required to pay you immediately, leaving you to believe I was the irresponsible one trying to inflict pain. No, Marv, it's time for a reality check.

"My last memory is of you in a new suit fleeing down the courtroom steps, unwilling to stop long enough for my dad to inquire as to the health of your sick father while I, in a dress I wore in high school, worried how I was going to finance my basic living costs plus pay you half of the farm's value per the decree. What you say now—that you wished me no harm—is what I want to believe, but sorry to say, that was not my experience.

"The fact that I immediately grieved upon news of your death is a good sign of my affection for you. However, the presence of hurtful memories is a sign I still have work to do to get rid of my buried resentment. My hunch is you'll find that true of you, also."

❄ ❄ ❄

Assuming that Marv is now on the other side, I asked Kym for a reading on my birthday, "Can you find him?"

K: Yep! Marv's over in the corner with a huge smile on his face. He just raised his hand and is moving forward. Marv stopped, turned around, and with a hand gesture waved for his parents to step forward, "Come on; come on." Both of his parents are with him now.

B: How nice. ... I want to say, "How nice to see you," but I don't actually see you or any other spirits except rarely for a second.

[*choking up*] Kym, I didn't tell you, but his folks, as a pleasant surprise, visited me several weeks ago. For an instant, I saw Jack dressed in his customary, dark business suit with crisp, white shirt and conservative, four-in-hand tie and Margaret in a stylish, turquoise, afternoon cocktail dress as silk, knee-length dresses were called in the fifties. Always a well-turned-out, handsome couple, I was thrilled to be able to see they still are. My vision of them faded fast, but we continued talking.

Even before our engagement, they always treated me as one of the family, especially when I was teaching in the small town where I was homesick for my family in Wisconsin and lonely for Marv away at college in the south. Hiking in the woods that surrounded the spring-fed lake was an activity I shared mostly with Marv's mother. Those walks were perfect for bonding and a happy escape from our respective jobs.

Their hospitality was always supportive, both during the years that Marv and I dated and throughout our fifteen years as a married couple. I couldn't have asked for friendlier, more welcoming in-laws. I'm happy to see they are still in my life.

M: [*jumping in with laser aim on our meeting's purpose today*] I always regretted not being the man I needed to be with you, more so than any of my other relationships. I knew who you were and I loved who you were, but I couldn't be the man you needed. My needs were very self-centered in what I felt

I wanted to give to the world. I could easily write it off to my youth, but I lived long enough to know that was just an excuse. I just wasn't the broad-shouldered man you needed. I always regretted that, but I never ever had one ounce of negative thoughts or feelings toward you. You were always so special in my heart; that's why I didn't come back to Michigan. I didn't want to upset you further after I baled out of our marriage.

B: Do you mean near the end of your life?

K: No, throughout your life. You were special to him in his heart over the years. I think he contemplated reconnecting, but he knew that was for selfish reasons.

B: And I guess I needed to go through that really hard time without a man in charge of me.

K: Beverly, don't confuse two different things. He's taking ownership of his failures; and he needs to tell you that. You're trying to let him off the hook.

B: Guilty! Yes, I was. I don't know what virtues he thought he sensed about me. When I think back, I was totally self-absorbed, too. I was not ready for the commitment of marriage.

M: Nor was I. But I saw what you needed and what I couldn't give.

B: To me that's extremely perceptive. I thank you for that insight.

M: If you believe it or not, you were a joy in my life.

B: Well, looking back at my old high school scrapbook recently, it was fun to revisit those happy memories. As far as contemporary questions go, now with you on one side and me on the other, I'm told by my spirit guide there are things that we could be doing to help each other at these stages of life.

M: I want to help you and be part of your support system. I myself am just beginning my journey over here; and you have such amazing people on your team, much more advanced than me and more understanding of the delicacies of this process.

My mother is elbowing me, "Us, too." [*chuckle*] Everybody wants to be a part of your little support system. These people are advanced; and I'm just starting. Can I, as I grow and change, help out?

B: Maybe. I have many kinds of relationships with the other people on the other side, but you and I have our own unique history. We can tailor-make remedies to clear us of our missteps in this life. Are there other specific things that you and I need or could do that would help each other independently?

M: I don't know because I'm not through my own process yet. I'm still dealing with my own life review and my own understanding of me. I'm looking at everything about me. But, do I have that hope? I would love to be able to work with you and see what else we can understand with each other but I can't say that because ...

Oh! Your spirit guide Samuel looked at me and indicated, "You can, Marv, when you're ready."

B: All I know is what Samuel has always said, "When you're ready." I suspect he means when we are both ready. I'm in the learning phase myself, but recognize this is a special, precious, specific time in our lives. I don't want to miss any opportunities if we can handle the issues.

M: You'll know when I come; you'll know it's me. As soon as I'm ready, I'd love to be a part of us helping each other.

B: Okay. Keep an eye on what Samuel suggests. Meaning no disrespect to your own spirit guide, I'm comfortable if you use Samuel as the overall guide on my timing.

M: Thank you for inviting us to your birthday party. Mom and Pop said, "Thanks, too."

B: [*tears*] My pleasure.

A few months later ...

Beverly (B), Marvin (M), Samuel (S)

B: Samuel, on several occasions I think about Marv and believe a lot of loving feelings are emanating from him. This morning I'm having that feeling again and thought maybe this is something we could talk about now.

S: Yes, go ahead with that idea. Your feelings of loving energy coming to you are definitely there and very strong. They are aimed at healing you, which I see they are definitely doing.

Marv is sending you those loving thoughts. You will be very proud to know how well he's doing. He's been quite an avid researcher; and we're very pleased with his eagerness to help.

First, I want you to enjoy that feeling. Second, I want you to share and reflect that loving energy back to the people in your life who you think have been lacking in those loving feeling for themselves. Now let me handoff to Marvin.

M: I'm doing fine; and I can do all kinds of things I never had any idea were available to me. I've been surprised and overwhelmed with the opportunities and the joy it brings. When alive, the churches I attended had no concept of what's going on after death. Yes, I can see a disadvantage of talking too happily about the other side. You don't want people coming over here before their time because they have come to Earth to do a job. It's important that they carry it out to the best of their ability.

I'm proud of you and Kym for working on this topic because people are not getting a very good idea of life on this side. You and Kym have a delicate job to find the right balance to encourage people—but not too much! [*laughter*]

B: Thanks for your encouragement. We feel it would be helpful for folks to know there is important work to be done wherever they reside. Likewise, I'm pleased to hear from

Samuel about your vigor in exploring the details of your life; and I wish you all the best.

M: I am indeed sending you loving thoughts because I want you to know I wish the very best for you as you complete whatever kind of work you are doing on the Earth plane before you leave to join us, which is inevitable—particularly at our ages. I'm not holding back at all because I want you to be as informed about my life as much as I can. I'm speaking to you with the tutelage of people like Samuel and my own spirit guide.

What I can tell you is I led a cautious life after leaving you. I was lost for a very long time and couldn't settle down. I taught out west but was neither emotionally happy nor finding fulfillment in my job.

B: [*struggling with weak reception*] I'm not sure I'm getting a clear message. I ask that my hearing improve or the connection be stronger.

M: Perhaps you're not sure you want to do this. I feel a lot of hesitation on your part. Do you really want to know? It's going to color how you think about me, even extending into many generations.

B: [*tearing up*] That's true. I want to know, but I don't want to know. I continually push myself into the question, "Is this something I can face now if it's going to help in the long run?" If you're picking up my hesitation, you're picking up Beverly's essence more than I even thought was there. The bottom line is to go ahead—but gingerly.

M: Which I will do because your guide is with me and helping me know what to talk about. You and I have talked a lot—when we each talk privately to ourselves in the "rolling ideas around in our head" mode. It seems we have found some peace between us. Over the years we individually have worked out our own personal feelings and hurts that we brought to our relationships. But now with this new telepathic form of communicating, we can see the other person's point of view and experiences in a brief, once-over-lightly way.

We can *start* to understand each other's pain, reactions, and disappointments in our relationship.

Bev, I want to know what it is I can do for you from this perspective because there are things from which I can help you heal yourself. I'll call them, *the mistakes in our marriage*. I'm still feeling like a newbie, but I will take your questions to Samuel and my own guide to see what we can come up with. Let's get to work here.

B: Are you able to explain this process?

M: No, not really. Apparently, I can't simply describe it. You need to ask questions that indicate you are ready for the information—so I'm told.

B: Oh man, it's that "Ask and ye shall receive." Sometimes I'm embarrassed with my questions.

M: Give it a shot.

B: Do you feel you're making progress? That may be a very intrusive question because there you are, I'm assuming, sitting with the very people whose job it is to help you make progress. See, this is part of my awkwardness.

M: It's awkward, because you're making it awkward. Just shout it out! Here, we don't accumulate feelings of blame. We just look at our life issues from a distant point of view. We're able to analyze things clearly without emotion.

B: Yeah, emotion is what gets us into trouble. Okay. ... So with this life, my dad had taken a plum job out of state. My parents and sister were now living in Wisconsin while I completed my high school degree in Detroit, staying with a friend's family. Then you entered the picture. The roles you and I played called for a crush on each other in our senior year.

Immediately after I graduated, we were confronted with separation. I questioned, "Do I rejoin my family or strike out on my own?" Either path I chose, I faced the opportunity to redo my life, shed the old, and welcome new adventures.

Instead, being realistic, I took the safe, secure choice and returned to my family, but I didn't embrace our family's new life in Wisconsin.

It took me almost four years to drop my grief over the loss of those life-affirming high school years. Instead, I played the martyr. I felt forced to live away from friends, without thinking how my parents were sensitive to the abruptness of the change for themselves and me. They did everything they could to ease my transition from high school life into college life. Sadly, I flunked the gratitude test.

I was slow to see the new opportunities. I chose to remain in my narrow mindset, deeply feeling resentful for several years before realizing that moving to a new location could be a wonderful opportunity to throw myself into a new adventure.

That's my take on one of many events presented to me for my growth. Perhaps you, Marv, were in a role to help me grow, but I didn't have the courage to cut the high school connection. The growth comes now in realizing I was a pouty, spoiled kid.

M: And I think the same way about my life. My parents did everything they could for me to have an easy life. That was the problem. I went to Michigan State and blew the opportunity because I wanted fun over realizing the opportunities, so I got kicked out. Grades were not my priority; yet, my folks made it possible to pick up the pieces and go to Auburn where I could live with my aunt and gradually start working my way out of that foolishness.

B: Then we both owe a debt to our parents who loved us and knocked themselves out in the best way they could to help us mature. Their motives were fine. Eventually, we've both arrived at the same understanding about opportunities that presented themselves and our attempts at solutions—but some a little late for implementation.

M: Yeah. I get your meaning.

B: Okay, Marv, what else would you like me to know?

M: You impacted me greatly for the rest of my life because I did such a poor job of being your companion and spouse. I felt badly about myself, so recovery took a long time.

B: This is hard for me to hear because I, too, am always telling myself, "I'm not good enough." I feel that is the response I have elicited in you right now. It was the same during the marriage and after the divorce.

M: No, I don't think it was like that. I knew I was a failure and missed an opportunity to grow with you. That's what I was running away from. During the period of time when we were waiting for the divorce, I visited my newly retired parents in Florida. They were very upset with me and urged me to go back, and as they would say, "Grow up and do your duties as an adult husband."

I could never muster up the courage to go back and face you. I thought you were unreasonably rough on me. I find, even now, you have a hard time recognizing how tough you were on me in terms of expectations of what I could do. That deeply hurt me. So I feel this urge to blame you for my slowness to recover. What do you have to say about that?

B: At the age of almost eighty, it's hard to get back into that mindset of fifty years ago. I don't know if I can tap into that accurately and quickly. I had tunnel vision for sure. I thought buying that Michigan farm was what I wanted—and a portion of what you wanted because I knew you'd be close to your family and life at that lake and golf club you loved.

Just as today, it's true I focused on an overwhelming To Do list. When I look at the photographs of you on the roofs of the barn and the house, I think, "Oh, my gosh! Here's a guy who's risking life and limb to do property maintenance." That was gutsy of you. It is part of helping me understand that I had not been giving you proper due at that time. I was expecting you to achieve my goals—like I am now, expecting Kym to stop everything in her life to write the books we're supposed to write together. I expected you to set aside your agenda to work on our property, which I realize now was not really your highest priority. Yet, buying a farmhouse near your parents *was* primary for you. If I made you feel inadequate, part of the blame is on me.

M: It's good to hear you say that, but I still think you are fudging the truth. I did a lot for you that you might not have been aware of.

B: I need to know such details. Nonetheless, I owe you an apology for under-appreciating you. It took a long time to begin to see my festering anger and communication shortcomings. May we continue in a few days?

M: Yes, of course.

Marv, who was not a direct man in life, is wasting no time to jump into the hard stuff. This discussion of events surrounding our wedding was continued a little later in the day:

M: I doubted that I was ready for marriage. I wanted it, yet I didn't want it. My preference was to wait because I didn't think I was ready for that kind of responsibility—yet. I was being pressured into it by you and friends who thought it was time for us to get married.

B: It's true; typical girl friends rarely missed an opportunity to urge each other to get married especially knowing the chances for meeting a mixture of eligible prospects became slim after the school years were over. *Better pick a guy while the supply lasts* is hardly a high-minded exercise, but it was rampant in the fifties. That idea was in the back of my mind, too, so I did apply pressure out of fear of being left behind. I was wrong on many levels and am owning up to it.

M: When the wedding date was set, I drove to Wisconsin with my parents. The eight-hour trip the day before the wedding was not particularly pleasant because I was getting all kinds of suggestions about how a good husband should treat his wife, what my responsibilities would be, and the seriousness of this step. Frankly, I had not given my husband role much serious thought despite our two-day preparation class. By the time we got to Milwaukee, I was feeling shaky about the whole business.

When I phoned to say we had arrived, your attitude was frankly one of resentment. You obviously were upset with the many unfinished details in the wedding preparations. That further upset me. I found myself wishing I could back out. So, we did not get off to a good start in terms of my feelings about marriage, my feelings about you, and beginning a life together. I'm sorry I wasn't in a better frame of mind, but I could hear you were not in a good mood either. It seemed we were on a train that had already been set in motion; and we had to stick with the ride. My recollection of the wedding day was a snowy, Easter afternoon in Milwaukee, which seemed like an odd omen and probably struck you that way, too.

That's how I was feeling. How were you feeling?

B: Yes, I was feeling the same way. My immediate family did not want me to marry you. The three of them had independently said so in their own soft manner as we approached the actual wedding day. So I knew how they felt. The crucial moment came to me just as the music started for me and Dad to walk down the chapel aisle. I hesitated. Dad spotted that.

Dad chuckled with resignation while muttering to himself, "It's too late now." The moment those words were out of his mouth, he cringed and thought it's not too late. It's never too late to say, "Hold off. This marriage is not going to work." He was angry with himself for saying it was too late. The decision was not yet irrevocable!

I realized I was afraid. Well, if we didn't get married, what was going to happen to me? I was going to embarrass my family and myself if I made a fuss and said, "Gee, folks, I don't think I want to get married after all." I couldn't see me breaking etiquette to do that. I also saw that I was afraid to break up—no matter who the groom was.

What would I do with myself? Where would I go? Where would I get a job? How would I conduct myself? Would I ever find somebody else to love me? All of those unknowns came tumbling down and buried me. Fear of the future sapped all of my courage. Frankly, I took the course of least resistance. But alas, against the wishes of the main characters in this drama, Dad and I walked down the aisle; and I got married.

I was so distraught that even when it came time to sign the legal papers after the ceremony, someone made the statement that the marriage wasn't official until the legal papers were signed. There I was, pen in hand, over the line where I was to sign to make it official, and frankly, I hesitated as long as I dared. Again I tried to muster up my courage. "Oh, I don't really want to get married. We're just not ready." Whether or not we'd ever be ready, I didn't have an answer.

Being afraid, wanting to make a good choice and a healthy decision for both of us—those were my feelings at the time. Not to act was strictly cowardice on my part. I failed to do what probably would have been best for both of us; and that was not to get married at all. That's where I am at this moment.

M: I think we are in agreement. We were too immature. To complicate matters, we were both people pleasers wanting to do what's proper and avoiding what would have been sensible and correct—for both of us to grow independently.

B: Yeah. I think that's the way I would sum it up, too. I don't have a clue at this moment if this is all new or if we are trying to undo something of the past. Maybe this is a good start and that's sufficient for now. I seem to be getting out of breath—my sign of increased stress.

M: I'm beginning to get some inklings of your stress too. In time, we may be able to work out things in depth. I think that would be good for both of us. I'm relieved that you are not upset with me feeling corralled into marriage. That's how I felt and wondered if you might have felt the same way.

B: Yeah, I think we're on board in understanding that people-pleaser trait in both of us. Taking the course of least resistance fits us. Yes, I think this conversation is a good start.

M: Yes. That's right. I hear you huffing and puffing which concerns me because I know these are the kind of things that hurt your heart. I want you to be well. I don't want to overstress you. So I will say goodbye for now and wish you all the best.

B: As I wish you, Marv. I think a great deal of you.

M: And you want to say you love me.

B: [*feeling the love*] Yes, that's right.

M: That's perfectly fine, because I love you a great deal. I regret we didn't meet when we were a little older and I was ready for marriage.

B: That goes for me, too. I thank you for talking to me and the fruitfulness of this conversation. Goodbye for now.

M: [*whisper*] Goodbye.

Roughly five hours later, Samuel instigated a chat:

S: Okay, Marv, would you like to step forward and tell Bev what's on your mind?

M: Yes, it's hard for me, but we've got to deal with it. The sooner we get rid of the unpleasantries, the better we'll both be. I feel I let you off the hook this afternoon. I really wanted to say more than I did, but I sugarcoated what I wanted to express.

B: Okay. What would you like to add or subtract from the earlier message?

M: To be perfectly honest I did not want to marry you. I felt like I was being ramrodded. Actually, I didn't want to marry anyone because I felt I wasn't ready. But, as you know, marriage was the next item on our agenda. Thinking back to those times, at our age we were all being funneled into a prescribed life pattern, which did not fit me.

Frankly, I was aware you were pushing and rushing me in that direction so I started to develop a resentment toward you. You were the person that I was attracted to during that particular phase of life, but not entirely by free will. According to the logic of the day, you were the person I was supposed to marry, but I wasn't sure about it because I did see that you were bossy. I sure didn't want to live with a bossy person because I had observed control-freaks in the marriages of my uncles and aunts. As you recall, both households were not happy places.

B: Yes. Both families were basically run by domineering females. I knew I was falling into that role but didn't have the skills to stop myself or help you learn to manage your life. You often seemed to be at a loss. Ironically, many times I thought of you as a child needing help. Was I really wanting a child to nurture and not a husband?

The event that really made me stop and think was when we were an engaged couple going somewhere in Milwaukee. I asked, "Have you got your car keys? The tickets? The directions?" As you left the room, Dad, who had witnessed my concerns, quietly asked me rhetorically, "Is this the way you want your life to be?"

That's when it really hit home—I was always going to have to play the role of organizer. I had never had that unwelcome thought before. I began to realize this marriage was going to be a mistake; but I didn't have the courage, strength, and character to say, "We need to have a talk about what we want in life. What are our odds of succeeding?" Unfortunately, it is hard for non-verbal people to have a heart-to-heart conversation.

I don't deny I got terribly bossy. Partly it was the role model I saw in my family. Mother dominated on the household front. I picked up her example of being in charge of keeping a household running in good repair and within budget. Fathers took care of all the other non-domestic issues.

The unfortunate part was that you and I never talked about doing what would be beneficial for both of us. I quickly felt I was operating in a vacuum. Starting in our first apartment, I was responsible for all meals, maintenance, laundry, and a full-time teaching job. Somehow the examples portrayed in our pre-nuptial class never stuck. Two afternoons in a group class was not long enough to break habits. Had we been honest with ourselves and each other, probably the best thing for us to do would have been to separate as gently as we could at that stage or get deeper counseling.

I would say I loved you then as I love you now. I can't speak for what was in your heart at the time, but I don't think I meant you any malice. With more maturity, more time, or living in a different era where society had changed a little, we might have avoided the hurt we ended up giving each other.

I don't know if there is any comfort in that. I hope there is. I don't say things out of meanness or unkindness; it's the way I remember it. I hope I'm fair to you. Is there something you want to say?

M: I need to think about it. This is going to take a long time for us to unravel because both of us are from the children-should-be seen-and-not-heard generation.

B: That's for sure! Our duty was to follow orders.

M: It was hard for me to talk then; and it took a lifetime to finally be able to *start* talking and expressing the things I think. I was not able to master speech in my life any more than you were able to master it in your lifetime. It's part of what you and I have to work through even now.

B: I understand, Marv. Take time to think about this. Let me know if I can help you or if you can help me clarify things. I want to be honest with myself and you. Continuing to kid ourselves isn't going to be productive.

Would you like to end this now? ... Okay, let me know when you are ready and able to talk again. Thank you, my dear. Goodbye. Thank you, guides, for the opportunity.

[*Marvin departs*]

S: Now, let me ask you, Beverly, before we disconnect, how do you feel about saying what's on your heart?

B: In some regards I physically feel a heaviness in the rib cage if that's what you mean. How do I feel emotionally? It gives me no pleasure. I hope I analyzed things accurately. I don't want to misrepresent myself or Marv. The expression would be, "I don't want to jerk him around." He deserves answers, kindness, and love—and forgiveness. We both need that; and for myself, I'm willing to offer it as a gift. Why would I not?

About a month later, I initiated a call.

Beverly (B), Marvin (M)

B: Today would be the fifty-seventh anniversary of our marriage, I wonder if Marv is interested in talking to me? It's totally up to him.

M: I'm ready, willing, and able to talk any time you are. I wish you'd get off this sad, lonely, depressed person you've become. I hate to say it, but I'm kind of ashamed of the way you conduct yourself these days. Maybe I didn't know you well enough, but I don't remember you being this introspective and introverted in all the time we were together. Maybe that was part of the problem that I didn't recognize soon enough.

B: True, Marv. I was always introspective but also more spontaneous and explorative in my activities when younger. I've let that disappear. People tend to be much more introspective when they are alone. I haven't figured out how to reinstall some of that fun stuff.

M: Well, that's all I wanted to say. I don't want you to pull me down, so I'm leaving.

B: [*thought but not uttered*] Perfect definition of a fair-weather friend!

Beverly's later reflection included:

Marv was a person who didn't have the foggiest idea of who I was when we met. He had built a life around a non-existent extrovert named Beverly. Even as a teenager my pensive, introverted side was profound; and I thought I recognized some of the same aspect in him. Apparently he chose to see only the other half of me—the graceful athlete.

Today, I'm amazed I didn't call him a selfish jerk, devoid of empathy, after that exchange. His self-centered comments hurt. Months later, I finally got it! Why didn't I defend myself by briefly enlightening him of the current challenges I was handling? Instead, I endured his crushing criticism in silence—another flaw to be added to my work-in-progress list!

A couple of days later I telepathically heard a voice and responded:

B: Would you like to go ahead this morning, Marv?

M: Yes, I'm greatly relieved to know you are doing better than the other day. It seemed that we, I and others, were really piling on you comments intended to be helpful, but we probably overdid it. I apologize for our harshness with you. Here, we tend to forget how difficult it is to control our physical and mental aspects when in the Earth body.

B: Yeah, your comments did give me a downer. Are you feeling okay?

M: Yes, actually I am. Thank you for asking and commenting on that. Currently I'm working on other relationships. I'm beginning to understand my parents' point of view; and it's wonderful to clear the air. Another reason for feeling better is clearing up some of my hang-ups.

Not surprisingly, you and I have similar hang-ups, so I encourage you to keep plugging away at them. It's not easy, but important. Even though you don't feel you're accomplishing much or feel you're going into the dumpster, any bit of progress makes a tremendous difference, particularly from your human viewpoint. Keep at it!

You and Kym, in some regards, appear mismatched, but any progress you can make with such extreme personalities is well worth it. I urge you to stick in there. I'm on your team and anxious to help you advance as far as you can.

B: Thank you for the pep talk. Having the typical mindset of our generation, I regret not being a more skilled communicator during our marriage. I wish you a successful journey and hope that your experiences before and after our divorce will ultimately benefit you as you progress.

M: Thanks. That was pretty much all I wanted to say.

B: Will you be able to keep touch with me?

M: Yes. We, of course, are linked. My understanding is we had several lifetimes together, many of which have yet to be resolved. So, I'm sure now, and when you pass over, we will still have many things to be worked out. I'm encouraged to know your loving feelings for me. I want you to do well and not be hindered by any contacts we've had together.

B: Yes, I feel that way about you, too.

M: If there is nothing else at this moment, I will say goodbye for now. But, I want to urge you to find more time to do pleasurable activities, Beverly.

B: Intellectually I know that, but unfortunately I find that tough because I enjoy my work. Thanks. My regards to your family.

M: Yeah. They do love you a lot.

B: I'm grateful. Say "hi" to our mutual friends. Thanks for getting back with me. I love you very much.

M: I know.

❋ ❋ ❋

In the next chapter readers will travel back in time to learn the backstory between Marv and Bev, which complicates their relationship even today because it is unfinished business.

Marvin  Chapter 2

November 28, 2018

From the kitchen this morning came the voice of Kym over the bubbling sound of coffee brewing, "The sorceress knows you want to communicate with her. She says you can be her scribe. Are you interested?"

"Interested? You bet I am!" was my reply from the living room.

But, Reader, first let me interject my mysterious backstory. Defined as one seriously studying the sciences, this sorceress is a past life of mine. Likewise, my husband Marvin, my sister Elaine, and my brother-in-law Larry, whom you will meet in their own chapters, each had key impactful roles in my life of the sorceress, now known as Beverly. If you like puzzles, you'll love keeping track of this cast of characters!

I'll immerse you in the storyline by listening in on Kym channeling a session for me in February 9, 2015:

Beverly (B), Kym (K), Samuel (S), Sorceress (Sor)

B: When I meditate, sometimes I see jewel-like colors of radiant clarity with abstract, undulating forms of bright green, blue, and magenta in my head. I see them now.

K: Your guide Samuel is telling me to do a healing on your heart with my right hand; and I saw it turn into a huge, many faceted diamond. As I move my hand around, the guides are showing me how amazing the color variations are inside the diamond.

I don't feel a negative hardening of the heart, but I felt a lot of crying when I first came upon it. I thought I was pulling up your current grief, but that doesn't seem to be the case.

B: Recently, I had a revelation that my heart had a lot of self-loathing. If that's how my heart feels, surely my soul is feeling rejected too. Now, I see brilliant green join the purple. Pure, sparkling, gorgeous gem colors. I also hear a voice say, "The soul doesn't hate you. The soul doesn't hate you."

K: Good! From my perspective I see only my hand in front of me holding an enormous diamond. I feel as if I'm going round and round like a spiral moving energetically up.

Oh, it dawned on me—I'm seeing old, gray, stone walls and steps. I'm in a castle going up to a turret with this beautiful diamond in my outstretched hand. My hand is vibrating hard, but I'm running to show somebody in the tower this enormous diamond. I think it's a sorceress.

Yeah, at the top, I burst through a big, wooden door which feels like a symbolic breakthrough of some kind! One small candle burns in the dark room, but the luminous diamond is shiny enough to lighten the round room.

I see a person in long, black gown and huge, black cape. I hear crying, but I sense strong, self-assured power! "Look at it," I tell the woman. She registers shock because she immediately recognizes it and is fascinated by this diamond. She doesn't say, "No. It's not mine!" Nothing like that, but I think the diamond is symbolic of something.

Having already seen it before, she stares at the diamond in my hand and says, "It's not what I expected. It's no longer the way I felt my heart would be." She expected an ugly, black, pulpy, icky, oozy thing, but now—actually seeing her own heart—she knows it's not ugly but stunning! I say, "See, it's not bad; it's not wrong; it's healed. It's in a huge diamond now. Look!" We both just look at the diamond. "May I have it?" she asks and extends her arms. I place the gem in her outstretched hands.

B: [*weeping*] Her description makes me cry. I'm feeling she has carried such a burden.

K: Sorceress, you've suffered so much. Don't burden your soul with punishment any longer.

She accepts her bright heart, which is as crystal clear as she wished it to be. Without opening her cape, she takes the diamond, folds her arms to her chest, and places the diamond in her body. It doesn't disappear. The heart diamond sits inside her body—I can still see it.

Oh! Sorceress, you've cleansed it; you've come back to the goodness of who you really are. Beverly, she's beaming now. She has accepted her punishment. Her purgatory, or whatever she put herself through lifetimes ago, has ended. Now she's cleansed and smiling back to me, "I'm back to being me."

[*sigh*] Beverly, that's why you were having trouble with your heart!

Oh my! The dark wood shutters at the windows that blocked out all the daylight in her turret prison suddenly blew open! Light beamed into the room and bounced off of her multi-faceted heart. The diamond lit up this entire enormous, beautiful round room filled with books, tables, and her favorite possessions. As punishment, the well-loved room had been in deep darkness with just a little candle for centuries so she couldn't enjoy her favorite things. "My self-imposed prison is now free," she said.

She grasped the edges of her cape, raised her arms and the fabric turned into feathered wings.

Turning into a bird, she flew out the window! I could see the big diamond in the bird's chest! Oh, my goodness, she's free! How lovely!

"Thank you for doing this for me," she's saying to you, Bev.

B: You're welcome. Thank you for being open to healing!

K: [*to Beverly*] Wow! This past life healing has impacted all her reincarnated lives between her sorceress life and your present life!

B: I have no idea when her sorceress life happened—when it all started except to be told it was five lifetimes ago.

K: I feel there's a shift. Your intuition was convoluted because of her lack of trust in her intuition. She blocked her spiritual insight because it betrayed her. So, she put up an enormous filter over her spiritual insight to deaden it. The consequence was that all her lives afterward were handicapped. Now you've removed that filter. I feel you're going to be able to trust your intuition and make decisions easier.

B: So the sorceress' pain and her filter are now eliminated from the experience of all the lives after her death in our reincarnation chain including my Beverly life?

K: Yes, she's removed the obstacle. And, she's removed the festering negative belief system of the sorceress that *she* believed she needed to suffer in order to pay her penitence.

B: And we really don't know much about her, do we? How painful it must have been for her all these years. Oh! I just heard applause. [*chuckle*]

K: It was for you. I see many hands clapping; I don't see faces. It's not just Timingo and Samuel. I think your past lives are happily celebrating their relief.

B: So what happens to the sorceress?

K: She's a beautiful, shiny, blue-black crow, flying around with an enormous diamond in her chest. That's how I see her. What a great symbol! I feel her release and joy!

B: I'm feeling numb right now. I don't know what to feel.

K: I'm sensing your soul went through a major shift that reconnected all your lives.

B: It's amazing my heart could look like a diamond! I remember a horrible experience not long ago in 2010. During a church service, I alone heard an ear-shattering shriek from my soul fragment collective. The sound was so frightening that I sheepishly looked around the sanctuary to see if anyone else was startled by the roar! Later, in a reading, I learned I was filled with self-loathing. The deeply mournful private sound came from my heart agonizing in pain over many lifetimes.

Wow! Now I'm realizing the loud moan went all the way back to the sorceress' self-loathing! It came from her, buried deep down inside me! Every life, including all her later lives, helped add another layer to that snowball of self-loathing. I, Beverly, have to take responsibility for unwittingly adding to that low-self-esteem mantra, too.

Recently, my guides told me to journal my feelings around self-loathing so I wouldn't forget the experience. With deep emotion I apologized to my heart as I went through tearful grief concerning my persistent, low self-image. Vigilantly my task now is to prevent any negative mindset each day.

K: Bev, the problems of the sorceress life have been erased. I'm asking your guide if there's any reason to go into that life again?

Your guide is saying, "Absolutely not!—not at this point."

No need; it wasn't the details that were important at this time. Sometimes the details can clutter up the significance. It was the bigger issues that needed to be cleared up—which you did.

B: Thank you, Kym. What a gift you gave me today!

K: Wait! I'm seeing a connection here. As punishment, the sorceress wouldn't let herself see her favorite things in her amazing turret room. Even if someone is in their beloved place, they can block out all enjoyment by becoming frozen in the dark alone.

B: How sad because she first needed to save herself. To be so disappointed in yourself that you close yourself off to everything is an extreme decision—a hopeless form of hell she created. In this case, Kym, you were the improvisational warrior breaking in the door. I thank you!

Over the next few years, more details revealed themselves. The following description by Kym is the sorceress reviewing her early life. She's looking down into the courtyard below through the wavy glass of a turret window.

Sor: As a beautiful, young woman, I dressed in a flowing, blue-green, floor-length gown with my curly, chestnut brown hair pulled back in each corner of my forehead. Our family all had the same rich hair color.

It was afternoon playtime. My two young girls, dressed in white with lace necklines and hems, were giggling, playing their own guessing game as I held my chubby toddler in my hands above my head. To pretend my son was flying brought us a joyful sense of freedom. All too quickly, he would have to take over the running of the property with all its intrigue. These moments of joy were rare enough. We were a beautiful picture of a youthful, energetic family, sharing some private moments of pleasure together.

But looking down at my younger self, I realize all that joy and happiness would soon leave me, and I would fall into despair because I couldn't heal my beloved son who held so much promise. I had to wait a long time for his birth. Beverly, just like you ordered your horse Rudy[1] to fit your needs, I ordered my son to have the requirements a man would need in a lifetime back then. My husband had been a disappointment; I always had to fill in the gaps he didn't handle. I was tired and wanted a helpmate son. I tricked my husband into impregnating me.

I no longer loved my husband. He had other interests and was never home. Therefore, I took care of our kingdom, while he became just a figurehead. He was lazy and never developed

---

1. As a youngster I designed my dream horse Rudy—right down to my horse's perfect round star on his forehead. Whimsically, I think I created him at that moment. Twenty years later I physically bought him. With his kindly temperament, he lived to be thirty-three and was a smooth joy to ride. Hence, I understand the sorceress' desire to create a perfect remedy to solve her problems.

his gifts, so he became afraid of my powers because I was successful. You have no idea what I could control; others didn't have my skill.

I was always on guard for my life and my family's life. My son was my joy, but it was short lived. The person you call Marv in this life was my son and a natural target for evil-intended people in those days. They knew he was next in line. They were clever and I relaxed my guard for a few moments. I suspected my son was poisoned by court dissension. The poor, little, lovely boy died a painful death; and I could not heal him.

I was in disbelief because I'd planned everything so carefully. I was stunned to be caught off-guard. I blamed my version of God and refused to communicate or ask for help. I thought I knew everything.

What I've learned from you is the concept of an outline[2]. Just like you, I had no idea such a force was at work in my life. I thought we lived our lives one moment at a time without there being a pattern or long range goal or lessons.

I didn't see how ugly and angry I was becoming after my baby died. I had no friend to confide in nor would I have been able to relax enough to take anyone into my confidence. I knew with my gifts I was special, above the masses. The less sympathy people offered me, the more I hardened myself against them and brought down harsher judgments in their lives. In despair I killed myself and my young daughters who I didn't want to leave alive in my dreadful world. I believed it was an act of kindness to let them die by my hand.

I went immediately into my turret hell. I cut myself off from everything—no growth, no ideas, nothing. This may make you angry, but I invented you, Beverly, so you would be haunted by me and never rest until you found me. You did as I designed. I knew you would find me and release me. Now, what do you think of me?

B: I still think of you as a person who needed a friend to help

---
2   See glossary

you work out your life's problems. But my comment may say more about my naïveté about your society. As for projecting all your problems into the future for me to solve, I'm not keen on that idea. Why did you dump it on me? What did that solve? It seems to me you've got to clean up your own mess; stuff you permitted to happen.[3] It's a tough concept.

Sor: Moving forward in time, did you think Marv (my toddler) abandoned you? Or, through understandable hardships did you abandon Marv? It sounds like abandonment is now a shared issue between you. I believe the two of you need to find peace on this matter. It sounds like my issue has been kicked down the road to be handled five lifetimes later by you folks.

B: And, what about those lives in-between the sorceress and Beverly? Those people need healing, too. And your daughters? I'm glad, Sorceress, you're stepping forward to get rid of the painful past. I applaud you and your courage. Please keep working on answers.

Sorceress, do you know you have spirit guides to help you? I do not fully know how this works, but you are not alone. If I sound overly critical about what looks like you delaying problem-solving efforts, I'm aware that I've done the same thing in my life. Perhaps you witnessed a few years ago the barrage of my negative past lives relentlessly attacking me wanting help. Regardless, you have an empathetic audience here. Do not fret; help is available.

K: Sorceress, tell us what we need to know about your life and feelings, because you're highly influencing your current life as Beverly! We'd like to help. Let's start with some basics. What were your talents and abilities? Did you have a lot of servants around? Whenever there are servants, they are listening.

Sor: We had too many servants around in that regard and never any privacy. As to abilities, I could do anything I put my mind to—that includes long distance astral travel and

---

3 After awhile, I softened upon reflection. Even today, how good am I at cleaning up my own stuff? Or, better yet, preventing a mess?

long distance healing by sending energy through my hands to someone or something else.

K: Could you read minds? Are you able to get premonitions on people?

Sor: Yes, randomly, but not consistently. People didn't trust each other in our era so they learn to cloak their thoughts.

K: Could you read the future for other people?

Sor: Yes, I could see the future pretty well if I focused on it.

K: Did people come to you for information on their future?

Sor: Sometimes, but I didn't particularly want people to know I could read them. Sometimes I made it look like I was just counseling them.

K: How about the past? Did you ever look into your own past to get clarity like we're doing with you?

Sor: I could look into the past, but I'm not sure if it ever occurred to me to look into *my own* past. I can't understand why, but I seem not to have been curious about that.

K: Let's go to healing. You had a sense you could heal people, but it didn't always manifest. You were unable to save your son's life. So that left you feeling unsure. Why did your powers not work here?

Sor: That's right. I'm not sure even now what I'm doing with my healing abilities. I would tell a person I thought I could heal him. But I'm not sure I really could. Sometimes I think I was putting up a big false front to let people think I was more powerful than I was. I was doing a lot of bluffing. When it didn't work, that left me disappointed because I thought I was doing everything right; yet, intended results didn't always happen.

K: Honey, that is so typical of our work with natural abilities. I have the same problem. Let me put that in perspective. As someone who is a *natural psychic*, it does feel like we are bluffing many times because we're not totally confident in our abilities. Nobody sat us down and taught us how to do something. We just seemed to know without knowing why we know. At times we question, "Am I just making things up?" Do you think you were having those self-doubts because your healing energy naturally came to you?

Sor: Yes, I can identify with what Kym's saying because those were my feelings, too. I was getting a lot of information but not a lot of confidence in the correctness of what I was doing.

K: Were you able physically to move things with your mind? Could you move a vase across a table?

Sor: Yes, because I could see the results right then.

K: What was your focus? Work or family? Were you highly involved in raising your children? Or was that left up to what we call a nanny?

Sor: I wanted to raise my children, but I wasn't really allowed to because I had so many official duties. My job was to keep peace in the kingdom. But how could I do that? I was shut up in the castle and not allowed to mingle. Safety was always a major concern because there were constant intrigues. I knew what dangerous times they were, but symbolically my hands were bound up behind my back. I couldn't do much.

K: Were you responsible for connecting with other kingdoms as a perfect party hostess?

Sor: My real job was to keep the wheels of industry and business moving rather than the social aspect. It was dog eat dog where people were fighting for work and positions—not frivolous stuff or the niceties of society. This was meat and potatoes, practical business.

K: So you had to make decisions based on which people came in and what they told you was happening in the kingdom?

Sor: That's exactly right. I didn't know who to trust. Sadly, my judgment was not based on experience.

K: Was it unusual for a woman to hold so much power in your era?

Sor: That's right, but my husband didn't want to do those things. He often disappeared, so it was left for me to do.

B: So you felt abandoned! Yes, I definitely know how it feels to fill a vacuum.

K: Yet, you held a lot of power. So this was your life prior to your son's passing where you were taking care of the daily matters of the kingdom and picking up your husband's shortcomings.

Sor: Yes.

K: Do you have any clue who poisoned your son?

Sor: I think I know who ordered it, but I don't know for sure, so I don't want to say.

B: [*feeling the sorceress' energy shift, an alarm was set off in Beverly*] May I jump in here, Sorceress? Are we talking about what you want to talk about?

Sor: No, not at all.

B: What is it you'd like to tell us? I want healing for both of us.

Sor: I want you to know that no peace will come to us until you and I decide what we're going to do about the future. I think you need to be much harder on yourself; I think you're lazy.

K: All right, we need to stop this! You're going in a direction that is not helpful to anyone, particularly Beverly, who is my main concern. We want to help you because that will ultimately help Beverly, but abuse to yourself or to Beverly is not going to be allowed.

B: We've done so much of that blame game already.

K: If that is where you want to go, Sorceress, it is not somewhere that's going to help Beverly or you. It's going to do the opposite. We're offering an opportunity to heal here, not blame.

Sor: I understand that, but I don't understand what you

expect of me. Am I not to express my anger?

K: You can express your anger but not at Beverly, who has done nothing to you. Hearing negative words is not helping. To tell you the truth, your self-loathing started the problem and it's now being played out in Beverly's life. If you want to become abusive, we refuse to join you.

B: My question is: isn't there someone who can help you? Kym, does she have guides?

K: [*slightly annoyed*] Everybody has guides, but she's still participating in her self-loathing and showing us exactly where she is not healed.

B: Step one is to know where you are hurting then, two, work your way out of it. Heal yourself.

K: We're setting boundaries, Sorceress. If you want to continue to have self-loathing feelings about yourself, we can't change that; but we will not let you place them on Beverly. It's neither fair nor warranted. She's working desperately to get out of that behavior herself.

B: Recently, have you been with me when I've been reviewing, step by step, my current life's experiences and memories? I have to go through my problems, my decisions, and find how I can fix them. We each need to do this work.

Sor: [*surprised*] I didn't know that was you. I thought I was experiencing somebody else who was trying to blame me for things I didn't know anything about.

K: Each life creates actions and consequences. Beverly has taken the time to review many parts of her life decisions and the consequences affecting her. But she's also coming into awareness that she is highly influenced by you, Sorceress—your unhealed parts, your self-loathing, and your loss of control in the grief over your son and its consequences. These problems are filtering through to her.

The thing is, Beverly is walking the walk. She's doing the work; and you need to do the work on your end about when you were alive as the sorceress. That's where the healing comes. This process is not there to "beat you up"; it's for you to look at it from a new point of view and say, "I did x, y, z when I was in terrible grief over the loss of my son." Once you're past that point, you can look back and realize, "I feel badly I did that, but I also find compassion for myself because I was grieving horribly without a support system."

Sor: It *does* make sense to me now. I will go back and start rethinking the events in my life and see if I can come up with some more creative thoughts.

K: We're willing to help you in the process.

Sor: But how?

K: By conversation. We can be the friends you didn't have back then—friends who can help you sort out this tragedy. It's exactly what I do for Bev and she does for me. We help each other to see events from different points of view.

Sor: And I can do that now?

K: Yes.

Sor: When and how can I do that?

K: We can set up a time to talk like we do with our guides. We make an appointment and just chat. It doesn't have to be long, but it has to go through Beverly. Sorceress, everything is perspective. Beverly has learned a choice she made in the heat of the moment at thirty years old is not the same behavior she would make at seventy-nine years old when she's outside of the drama. Emotions are what make us get out of character and do wacky things.

You were living in survivor mode during a highly emotional, scary time. You couldn't trust your servants, your husband, and were so psychic you sensed things before they manifested. Then you didn't get a warning your son's life was in danger, which was another blow. You have unnecessarily beaten yourself up for not seeing, knowing, or preventing that calamity.

Sor: And what about him?

B: Who do you mean? Your son?

Sor: No, that other person who's standing with me right now.

K: Sorceress, can you identify him?

B: Could you ask him his name?

Sor: He says his name is Samuel. He's asking me to ask you to introduce me to him.

B: [*relieved*] I can say this: Samuel is the name of my spirit guide. I'm going to assume that this Samuel is the person who has been helping me and who, perhaps in the past, was helping you. Apparently not having officially met, you were unaware there was such a person, who helps you and me, in our respective lives. So, Sorceress, I would like you to meet this person I call my spirit guide, Samuel. Tell me what you sense about him.

Sor: Yes. I see him; and I recognize him from the past. He was my friend, but I didn't know who he was or remember his name. He says he would like me to go with him now and see what we can learn together. He's asking for your blessing in this event.

B: Yes, of course, go. I'm happy to have you meet Samuel because I have found him to be a wonderful friend.

Sor: We are going to leave now. We will be in touch. Samuel will take charge of you and me—the three of us.

B: I'm thrilled. This is a good thing to happen. I wish you well!

K: Thank you. Beverly, that's the place for her to go; you introduced her to her guide. Great!

❅ ❅ ❅

Beverly (B), Kym (K), Samuel (S)

S: Beverly, you're like most people. In some lives you are so critical of yourself that you create a hell. When you were the sorceress, in death she locked herself up for a punishing five lifetimes. On February 9, 2015 you and Kym were at the stage where you could actually release the sorceress from her turret hell by breaking her illusion.

B: Yes, I'm touched by that event. And now she's on her own?

S: Released from that illusion, she's now continuing to work on her problems.

B: I thought it was my task to be working on her stuff.

S: You work on it *with* her. You're helping her. You've consciously joined forces now.

B: How would we say this? She still has her own personality; she didn't melt into me.

S: Yes, because you're conscious of each other, you have joined forces. On some level you merged. Nonetheless, it is her stuff—developed in her particular life, her behavior, and her consequences. She's not off the hook. It's not all being dumped on you to heal her. She's still working her own life except now you're standing next to her. You're both deciding, "Okay, I deal with this; you deal with that."

B: So I was wrong! Working together is a new idea. Before, I thought only I was responsible to heal myself for the benefit of all in my "chain." Actually that ball's still in her court.

K: Yeah, I never saw that before, either. Our past lives are still working their stuff, but you're helping. Ultimately they are of you so you become a team. Every time we become more conscious in this life about our past lives, we present them a healing opportunity.

A full year later:

Beverly (B), Kym, (K), Samuel (S), Sorceress (Sor)

K: Beverly, for this updated reading to focus my attention, I need to see again the sorceress playing in the courtyard with her children. ... Seeing a transparent son indicates her youngest child doesn't live. Since she was devastated by his poisoning, the slippery slope of her power problems started. Her intense mourning and her anger at the world encouraged her to make bad choices as her heart hardened and turned her into an unhappy, bitter woman. Whether she did not use her power to help people, or she used her power to bring about the demise of folks is uncertain, but I feel some deaths came from decisions she made.

B: But she came into that lifetime to go through that experience, having worked out her outline in advance. Right?

K: Yes, but she didn't consciously know that. She said she "let it best her." In that era, early death of children was commonplace. "Get over it; move on" was society's attitude. Folks didn't suggest, "You ought to get some help." Since she was in a powerful position buried in her own grief, the more unhappy she was, the more miserable she made other people under her domain.

I feel I'm at the same window as the first session looking down at her young self, playing and laughing with her three kids. With china-white, smooth complexion, she was beautiful. But, now I'm looking at what appears to be an old, crabby lady as she saw herself.

B: That would hurt.

K: Yes. Sorrowful and dark is how she remembers her life.

B: So she took her own life. How sad.

K: Yes, when she was in her twenties.

Sor: I couldn't take it anymore. Looking back on my life, I can see myself being overtaken by the darkness, the grief, the loss, the anger, the resentment, and the bitterness. I had already made many decisions that killed many people.

Now that I have been released from my hell illusion, you can witness my thoughts. I can look at my life from a different point of view. When the windows of my turret flew open,

I saw tons of books and instruments for measuring. At the time of my death, I was studying and harnessing the power of innate, natural abilities and how to use them. These abilities were not so rare. My family had great powers; a brother who levitated, a mother who could make balls of fire. I had a lot of these same abilities, which I worked with and became a master.

Since I have connected with you, Beverly, I changed and came into new awareness of why I did what I did, but not in judgment. When you're squeezed into a judgment box, all you can see is everything you did wrong. Now I can look at how I got there. Many people go down the path of self-destruction after the death of a child, like I did. I'm not in those emotions any longer and can see more clearly. Eventually forgiving myself will help.

B: She is on her own to move freely. In a way, she's doing her life-after-life review. She and I can help each other. It's a very complex notion.

K: I'm having trouble trying to pull away from the sorceress now so I can move on to other topics. Sorceress, move out of my system because all I feel is your pain. I want to stop seeing you down in the courtyard with your kids.

Sor: Please, don't leave.

K: All right, Sorceress, what do you want me to tell Beverly?

Sor: I want to talk about her dark feelings.

B: Is she the source of my feelings of heaviness?

K: I don't know yet. She's trying to focus me on those dark feelings you were having in the past. These are your true feelings that have been in your head, not when you were just trying to get some ghost off of you.

Sor: Around the divorce, loss of your farm, and the loss of your horse Rudy, these thoughts are really a much larger part of you than you allowed yourself to remember. These feelings are *not* new; they are just newly coming back to your awareness. These are keys to a lot of your buried depression. You have many things swirling around in your head, but you don't take time to pull out any one thing and study it.

The same is true with me. Unaware that the loss of my child caused me all these feelings, I stuffed them down inside me. I might have done better, but there was no other support system available. I tried to shove them down and move on, but emotions crept up and ate away at me. I ignored the cause of the feelings, so I got more and more angry. I don't want you, Beverly, to do this with the tough times of your life! You're really good at blocking out things you don't want to believe or confront.

B: I'm aware of this connection and how we're affecting our soul fragments when they're going through a bad time. I'm starting to say to myself, "Is this something I originated? Or, is this one from my fragments? Or a past life? Then [*chuckle*] I find myself apologizing to all my associates if it's something I originated and am the one sending out hurtful vibes. Yeah, I've always had that underlying dark, negative ...

Sor: Yeah, it comes from me—allowing the avoidance of problems to overrun everything.

B: Yes, at least, now I have a little bit of a handle on understanding how sadness radiates out through all my soul fragments.

Sor: It has lightened up simply because I've gotten you to talk.

K: She's taking responsibility for depression filtering down through her soul fragment chain.

B: But how does she get rid of it?

Sor: I'm working on it now by supporting you and everybody else in my chain. You all need to find the core issue. If you go with what you just said, when you start to feel depressed, ask, "Does this originate with me in my life right now?" If it is this life's garbage, then deal with the issue. When it's not this life, you have to assume it's somebody else's stuff. Since you don't know whose it is, take it off of your shoulders and put it on the shelf for someone else to handle. You're not adding to it. Send prayers and healings, but leave it for the owner outside of you.

Discernment is something I didn't have either. If I had, I would have known, "I'm grieving; I'm mad at the world because I had no control over the death of my son." If I had known that, misery wouldn't have infiltrated every part of my life. You and I know better now because I'm outside the emotion of it.

Don't keep beating yourself up. If it's not yours, let it go. If it is yours, go to the core of the issue and fix it. You have a tendency to let it affect every part of your life. Beverly, unfortunately, you're following in my footsteps.

Samuel: [*comforting*] This is just a hiccup in your life. It had its purpose. Beverly, keep finding your power. Humans continually get caught up in the details of their past lives and forget to focus on the main points. We guides want you to concentrate on your life goals so you can avoid repeating unpleasant experiences.

I will use that streamline approach here. What you can continue to learn about the sorceress life is how she got to where she was—how she got to self-condemnation. If there's anything you can learn at this point, it is to catch yourself! Stop yourself when imitating her behavior because she didn't! She started down that destructive road like a train gathering steam.

She had an extreme experience. You don't. But it's not the experience, it's the behavior! In her life she made some tragic decisions. Her ego overtook her. You haven't had a situation where you made a tragic judgment that took lives. But your behavior is the same! It's as if you *did* make an unwise, deadly decision because you're so hard on yourself!

Sometimes we guides don't share details of a situation with you because we don't see how it will help you. In this case, it's the similar behavior you continue to repeat which is why we wanted to talk about it.

B: Thank you for the direct answer and the reasoning behind the answer! So, your message is stop bad mouthing myself?

Samuel: Exactly, that's what you have to keep relearning! Don't repeat her self-criticism. It's not just Beverly beating up herself; it's sorceress still beating up herself or her behavior is being incorporated in you. So you're working, too. You're working her issues and yours and your other soul fragments.

❄ ❄ ❄

In the next chapter, you're invited to witness some sessions that allowed Marv and me to begin clumsily to heal even though we are on different planes. Obviously, we want to understand, then jettison, our debris so we can go on as friends who shared an intense relationship once upon a time.

Marvin — Chapter 3

Earlier, when I went to see the energy worker, Susan Gibson, she discovered my physical heart problems were related to Marv. I learned there are many practical steps I can take to work through my Beverly marriage—like a therapy session. When I relayed this quandary to Kym, I wondered what she would channel. The fact that I'm still enmeshed in my sorceress life will probably come up.

Beverly (B), Kym (K), Samuel (S)

B: Kym, do you see a connection between my physical heart and Marv? If so, what can Marv and I do about helping each other now? If Samuel could give some clarification, I'd be appreciative.

S: You did not deal well in the past and current lives. The broken heart of the sorceress was caused by the demise of her son. This infant became your husband Marvin in your Beverly life. Therefore, you had an extra hard time dealing with losing Marv in this lifetime through divorce. Your emotions are all enmeshed in the unresolved feelings of you as the sorceress losing her baby and further complicated by Beverly losing her husband.

B: It probably hurts all the more because I pushed aside my feelings of Marv's rejection by stuffing that divorce stigma away in my mental cold-case file to be thought about later when I could get to it.

K: Yep. Well, *later* just arrived! Marv was your son when you were the sorceress.

B: How do I remedy that on Earth in my current life?

K: You need to understand her (you) from the past. The lady had a huge issue around depression and melancholy but didn't deal with it successfully. To get angry was easier than to deal with the emotional issues around the murder of her beloved son. Her hostility caused damage to innocent people's lives. It was easier for her to take out her frustrations on everyone else. It was too tender, too much for her. Not until she saw what damage she caused was she able to say, "I can't be left with my psychic abilities. I'm using them wrongly because of my own grief. I must remove myself."

B: Was there no grieving husband? Had she no friends to help her sort out these things?

K: He was off either fighting or pursuing other interests. I don't know what his issue was, but she didn't have any real friends in which to confide. Even with three kids, I feel tons of loneliness. When her son died, she was left to her own devices. But for her, she loved this little boy on such a deep level that she felt tremendous loss—particularly since she had invested so many hopes in him.

With the target of her grief aimed at other people, the sorceress didn't heal; the misery compounded. Now you, Beverly, have to deal with it! She reincarnated eventually into Beverly with your soft elements of compassion; in fact, you have been overly compassionate in how you try to live your life. In five lifetimes, see how you came from strong sorceress traits into weak ones to deal with big issues. Sadly, Tender Beverly couldn't deal with them properly either, because Beverly had so many losses (death of parents, loss of job, marriage, and friends) in such quick succession that you couldn't cope. The sad way your relationship ended with Marv is an example.

B: Is it hurting Marv now because he deserted me in a prior life when I was his sorceress mother? As his wife, I was loyal to him; yet, he didn't reciprocate with flexibility in his role as my husband.

K: You didn't know he was your son from your sorceress life. Your soul knew he had played that role and was emotionally connected to him, but you, Beverly, weren't aware. The sorceress experienced a form of abandonment by him being her murdered child. It was not his choice to leave her. Now he returned, but he deserted you (her) as a husband. His role was different, but equally devastating!

B: Since we planned our lives in advance, what did we hope to gain? Our outlines would have been mutually agreed upon. What's in it for Marv? What's in it for me? What's in it for the sorceress? Where do we go from here?

At first Marv was doing some of the heavy repair of the barn roof, painting the house roof, and really some dangerous stuff. I took too much for granted. I thought, "We bought this farm; work is just part of the package." Maintenance was not part of his world, nor was financial planning. Building a future had little appeal.

I know I did not treat Marv very well in terms of giving him the respect that was due him, because, frankly, I wanted a workaholic husband. He was, but his love was directed at things he was interested in, which is good and proper, but not necessarily at the things I treasured.

K: You wanted someone who would be a partner to you in the same interest areas.

B: Yes. For me it was home, art, and horses. Marv was into track and swimming. I have no problem with both of us being interested in something and energetically pursuing it. However, we both assumed our partner would be attached to our own personal passions to some degree. That idea expresses our immaturity for marriage in my opinion. I found I wasn't ready to surrender half of my life to be his helpmate if he wasn't willing to be mine.

K: He did the heavy lifting labor, but what about all the other farm and household stuff? Did you take care of that work?

B: Yes, I handled vegetable gardening, canning, meals, haying, horse tending, painting, housekeeping and maintenance—totally exhausting. Purchasing a push lawn mower went to the point of being absurd!

K: Looking at the sorceress' life through a toddler eyes, he feels like a three year old with expectations of a life that would give her stability, joy, and whatever she wanted. He would cuddle and adore her, but that expectation ended for her when the child died and could no longer supply hope and love.

Looking at the Beverly life, your expectation was Marv, again, would become a partner with you. However, he wasn't reciprocating enough by working toward a long-term partnership. The real appeal of buying that farmhouse was the close proximity to his parents living two miles away on the lake with swim team opportunities. Surprisingly, that put you in the positive column.

B: The proposed move put me in his favor because of the location. Conversely, it saddened both my parents and me to know I would be living four hundred miles away and would rarely see them. Yet, they were joyful about me taking steps to make another of my dreams come true with horses. These are all heart things; aren't they?

K: Yes, you were broken hearted by your thwarted expectations—even as the sorceress had been. There's more to a relationship than just "he died" and "my heart is broken." The Sorceress' desires were foiled and betrayed by his death. I'm sure parents don't blame a child for dying as if it's the child's fault. We sometimes fault our husbands or siblings for dying, but we don't tend to blame children. Nonetheless, you were mad at the fact you were without him in both cases.

B: Because it's impinging on *my* dreams.

K: Yes. She could probably never verbalize to the child how she was angry that he left her. But, in essence that's what's going on. She/you stuffed the anger down.

B: To the *now* part: My question is what can we do to help ourselves?

K: You never processed it. Now go back to your 1950s mindset. So let's not go to today's perspective. You never gave voice to the youthful Beverly at the time! You've got to go back there.

B: As the sorceress?

K: No, not that far back, yet. You have to deal with your marriage. That young Beverly who didn't address her feelings needs to dredge up and give voice to her feelings! At that earlier time, she immediately moved into survival mode.

Think of her; put yourself back in her shoes. You're that young woman who loves her farm, sees its potential, and takes care of the everyday workings. Your husband doesn't; his dream has changed. When he leaves her, he is entitled to fifty percent ownership of the one thing she has, her dream. She wants to keep the farm; she wants to buy him out.

She goes right into survival mode because her feelings are too intense. Remember, both things are true: she is, and you are, the sorceress. She's also feeling, "My baby, left me—again!" Her dust is all stirred up again. So unbeknownst to you, you're dealing with her weak spot, which you didn't want, but it was easier for you to move into survival than to deal with her, and your, buried hostility, "I'm really angry at you!"

Your parents had a good marriage. You were expecting the same. Now all of it was shattered! Marriage was expected of girls in your era, not divorce. You were dealing with a lot of compounded social pressures and your own fantasies. It was too hard for you to deal with those issues; you chose to concentrate on the practical daily problems first and worry about the other stuff later.

B: How do I deal with that now?

K: Your biggest need is for young Beverly now *to be heard*. You have to give her a safe place through journaling. How did

Beverly feel? Let her talk. Go back to who she was and say, "How did you feel about this?" It's time to let it out. You can't keep stuffing your feelings down anymore. Automatically it's going to lead to your feelings before the marriage failed, because the marriage was not fulfilling. It was not a partnership.

When you got into it, the marriage wasn't that great. He was never around nor really interested. After moving to the country, to survive in life you put your love into the farm not the marriage. You need to go back and dredge that up to release it.

Review the feelings of young Beverly starting from your family's concerns about Marv to your early marital distress when you realized your family was right. Now look at the marriage. It kept getting worse because Marv wasn't working at it. The space between the two of you grew bigger. All of a sudden he left a note on the dining room table stating he has left you.

Now you have to deal with saving the farm by finding money to buy him out and covering basic daily expenses and any debts he compiled while waiting for the divorce papers. Basic survival. Then, you have to tell your parents you were wrong about choosing your marriage partner. Your mother looks alarmingly sick and unexpectedly dies shortly thereafter; and then you're reeling from her suicide. Now dad's sick. At the same time, you're trying to learn and revive an old roller-shade business opportunity. Stretch out all those blows and get young Beverly to talk about how she felt during all that upheaval.

B: There was so much going on all at once; and I had to decide everything quickly.

K: And you're not a quick decider so that must have been stressful for you.

You have to look at the marriage, the feelings around Marv and the loss of him as a friend with whom you had good times. Things change. On top of all that, you're not thrilled with your professional choice of teaching since you were constantly burned out with that occupation.

B: I'm an artist, I didn't wanted to be a teacher and felt trapped professionally. My talent painted myself into a tight corner.

K: You want to know how to fix this. Well, you can't fix this here because you haven't let these issues come to the surface yet. You have to do this emotionally expressive part!

B: You mean I have to sit down and write it?

K: But not from a "this is what I did wrong" point of view. Explore what the situation was. What was he doing? What was I doing? How were we overcompensating? You were loving different things: the farm, the house, and the horses. What was he loving? He was loving his students, the swim and track meets, and traveling with them to open their lives to new possibilities. You both were getting your love fulfilled on some level by separate activities. The problem was neither of you were putting a focus on marital love to keep that going.

This *isn't* an opportunity for you to beat yourself or Marv up. State what happened. Next, allow young Beverly to voice how she feels about this. Next, you've got to tell your parents how this young Beverly feels about telling them they were right, "Marv and I were not ready for marriage." You need to express completely whatever young Beverly's thoughts were when she came home to find a departure note from Marv. Then, how did her parents react to Marv filing for divorce? How did young Beverly feel about their reaction? Give her a voice. You've only looked at the big pieces; you must look at the little pieces that affected you, too.

B: Those are the things that hurt, aren't they?

K: Yes, I see your heart as one big oozing sore filled with pus. You've got to go in and push on those parts. Release that pus. Your poor heart has been holding all this stuff. It's holding the sorceress back, holding the Beverly back; and it hurts.

The sorceress is the one needing the healing, but you can't get to her until you finish with Beverly. Bring up everything young Beverly lost including your unresolved feelings around your mother's death. Your dad, and your sister lived through her suicide as survivors. You have, yet, to face this sensitivity, too.

There are other feelings in there—all broken hearts of yours. Marv's divorce broke your heart, your mom's suicide, your dad's death broke your heart, your sister's illness broke your heart. Losing your horse Rudy and eventually selling the farm broke your heart.

Only after all that, can you give voice to this sorceress. It started with your sorceress and her broken heart so you, Beverly, came into this life already having a devastated little heart. You then contracted heart injuring rheumatic fever as a child, which physically put the icing on this cake, so to speak.

Once you have dealt with the Beverly pain, you can let the sorceress talk about what it was like to have her favorite child murdered. She will be able to talk, because she won't have to talk through *your* garbage. You've pushed your trash all out of the way, giving her the space to release her pain, too. Sadly, up to now, she wasn't heard and you weren't either.

B: I didn't realize there was so much. Maybe my writing needs to start with meeting Marv as a senior in high school.

K: That's why it's so important to write it down in order until now when you're seventy-nine. He was pretty pivotal in your life. Now finding out he was your child ...

B: A child in whom I had so much hope. Now, I've got the same disappointments.

K: But more so, because he wasn't a young child who died, he was an older guy who hurt you.

B: So, is that connected to things I can do in this life? In other words, is there an advantage of him being on one side and me being on the other?

K: I already feel it's helping him to change because you've come into that new piece of knowledge. He was your son; he was your husband. They are connected. I feel like something in him is healing because you're going to work out those two lives.

Take care of the physical parts; but it's the emotional healing that's the most profound for you, Beverly. The emotional side will heal your heart issues.

B: To be frank, I've felt like my heart's diagnosis is a death sentence.

K: Well, it is. A broken heart is all about the people you lost in a short period of time. Your sister's Parkinson has to be in there because you watched her body betray itself ...

B: Yes, and additionally, what seemed to me her passivity in her marriage broke my heart, too.

K: Is it a mirror to what your marriage was like?

B: Not really. Marv left, but Larry would imply, "I'm the man; I'll decide everything."

K: It drives you crazy. Things that drive us crazy usually are a mirror to us, showing us things we need to work on—though not always exactly the same way. Did Marv pull the "I'm the man" attitude in some ways that were very difficult for you to take?

B: I suppose abandonment is "I've decided to leave." My choice.

K: So Marv wasn't like Larry who made everyday decisions that wore others down. Were you pretty much independent to make your own choices?

B: Yes, Marv was quite the opposite; he was the procrastinator. I paid the bills on time and kept the life stuff organized otherwise it would never be handled.

K: When did he pull that "I am the man" card?

B: Around 1975 before the divorce, he mentally had already bailed out of the marriage. "I'm taking the track team to St. Louis this weekend." Commitments were made before I knew there was a track meet planned.

K: No discussion. You weren't a team even on that level. He'd make a statement; and you were expected to live with it. That's the maleness of "this is what I'm doing." Did you do that to him?

B: Probably—like I do to you, not talking ahead of time about what I'm planning. I think, "This will work out, I can do this without upsetting anyone's plans." All carefully organized in my head but not a good way to communicate. However, this was the best I could muster to fill my needs.

K: So you didn't talk to him about it.

B: Talking was hard for Marv. His family talked courteously, but always came up with intricate, evolving plans that needed frequent revision, keeping everyone confused and rattled trying to plan their day.

When Marv visited my family, by contrast, it was the opposite. Someone would put an idea on the table of what to do for a family outing for an afternoon. The person suggesting the idea had roughly figured out the feasibility of the idea. We would all consider our interest and accept or reject the suggestion. By gentle nod or a nay or yea vote, the suggested activity was selected and decided quickly. I never felt handicapped or inhibited other than I was the littlest kid.

When Marv was exposed to that kind of fast decision-making technique, and we had decided to, for example, go to the beach that afternoon, he was upset. "How come I wasn't asked my opinion?" "Well, you were sitting at the table when the suggestion was made and voted upon. I saw you nodding. Why didn't you chime in with an alternative outing instead?"

Marv was convinced decisions were made in his absence. They weren't, but they were different from the open-ended, never-ending planning routines Marv's family engaged in. It was hard to merge two such different styles in a marriage just as it was in a business relationship.

K: The big block of unresolved issues around Marv is a key issue. It's where you went against how your parents saw things and their desires. Then you're dealing with guilt around admitting that your family was right about your spouse selection. This ending stopped everything: Marv divorced, your mother died shortly thereafter, and your father was handling overwhelming grief, as was your sister.

B: Like a huge log jam just broke and came tumbling down on me ...

K: That's what you have to deal with now, because emotionally you didn't deal with this trauma then. You were too much in survival: Okay, mother died; what do Elaine and I have to do? Dad's getting sick; what do Elaine and I have to do? How do I take care of myself and the farm while working part time at the church?

B: I had started my historic drapery business and realized I couldn't easily do that from the Michigan countryside. Rudy my horse was dead by then. Inheriting Uncle Art's house in Ohio was an opportunity I couldn't pass up. I thank Elaine for sitting on the back porch with me as she helped me weigh the pros and cons of moving to Cincinnati.

K: Let's compare lives. In order to help the sorceress deal with her family loss, her next life was based on the last life. She didn't deal with the loss of her son and other matters at all well. Because she hurt other people following the death of her son, she said, "I'll come back, but I won't come back with any powers because I've got to deal with this huge heartache that caused all my powers to go awry. I wasn't dealing properly with my heartache." Now it's time for Beverly/Sorceress to deal with the emotional part of it.

B: What is the emotion of it? I sure did my share of crying.

K: Look at your life from the mature Beverly point of view. Write it down. This is the situation from a non-emotional view: this is where we were living, this is what was happening to the marriage.

Then, hand the pen over to *young* Beverly. What did young Beverly feel about this situation? Let young Beverly write her feelings about her life. Letting each Beverly answer will allow your intellectual side and your emotional side to describe both aspects.

B: I certainly fell into a bossy stage before we bought the farm when I realizing Marv didn't want any part of running a household. I had expected that he would change when we switched from apartment renting to home ownership. But I discovered I was still always left to fill the vacuum. I thought, "Oh well, I guess I have to become one of those bossy wives who make me cringe." The idea made me mad.

K: You might write many scenarios of the early part of your marriage. This is one; this is another. Let young Beverly say all she wants to say. Don't correct her! Don't shut her down from expressing what she needs to say!

B: Yes. I was arrogant—so much so I even thought, *What do my parents know about love?* I ignored the fact that as a unit, they had survived the tension of the Great Depression and World War II!

K: Look at what expectations you had. Let young Beverly answer.

B: Even Marv's mother forewarned me as I got to understand what her life was really like. She was exhausted and not happy with life as a housewife while also being employed outside the home. Publicly she was a pretty ornament but privately an overworked draft horse, not sufficiently respected by her loved ones.

K: Right. She raised that kid and knew what his home life was like—all that thoughtlessness. Why did young Beverly ignore all this information in plain sight? What motivated young Beverly?

B: Was it my Aries, bull-headed "I'm going to do it my way. I'll show them! I can make things work!"? In some regards I did, but I wasn't having much fun. Thus, as Elaine always said,

"Marv did you a favor by getting up and leaving."

K: Yeah, because you wouldn't have gotten up and left.

B: Correct, I wouldn't. I thought it was my duty to honor my wedding vows—especially with my Christian background. You certainly don't divorce! If you make a mistake, tough it out. It's another aspect of the cold, unforgiving view of God found in most churches of the 1950s.

What if Marv and I had not separated? I would now suddenly be free at age seventy-eight as he died in November. What would our life have been like? I would be bitchy and grouchy. Maybe I'd become another version of the latter sorceress. Marv would do his hobbies; and I would try to avoid contact with him.

My biggest dishonesty to Marv and myself as I entered the marriage was I knew I didn't want kids, and surprisingly said so. I thought in time I would magically grow to want them, but I never reached that state of mind; in fact, as marriage grew harder, I wanted them less. I felt the air was being sucked out of me. I realized my husband would be the oldest kid in the pack.

K: Wow! As soon as the other side said, "Marv was your son." You were determined to have him again in some capacity during this life.

B: Because he is the happiness of my sorceress life, we're going to prove it; we're still going to set the world on fire! Son of a gun, that never happened!

K: Okay, so in developing your new Beverly life outline, you determined he would come in, but as your boyfriend then husband this time around. Your needs were still to have him, which you really didn't have as the sorceress. (I got a chill all the way down my back). You get the picture. Let's call it a day; you've got a lot to process, Bev.

❄ ❄ ❄

I woke up the next morning wondering about yesterday's

channeling session trying to sort through the information about the sorceress, Marv, and me concerning our three-way relationship. How can we untangle our mutual experiences to find peace, understanding, and forgiveness between us? Not surprisingly, Marv popped into my head—but he wasn't alone.

Beverly (B), Marvin (M), Unknown Voice (U)

B: Marv, you are with somebody who is a stranger to you at this moment. Is that true?

M: Yes, I'm with lots of people who are strangers to me.

B: [*seems to be an open public class*] Would someone like to come forward and speak?

U: Here. My name is not important, but I see the two of you are struggling. You haven't even started by saying you love each other and want the best for each other. I have not heard those words come from either of you.

M: I am here only for that purpose and none other. Before we made a formal connection, I heard Beverly say that was her intention. I know that was sincere and communicated between us without your presence. So, don't fear those words were not expressed. I don't think either one of us is communicating for any kind of show, but as an honest expression of how we feel about each other. I'm glad you brought that up so we could clear the air. I know she loves me and I love her. I know she has felt the depth of my love for her; and I have felt the depth of hers towards me. Don't make judgments on just what you see.

B: Thank you, Marvin, for standing up for us. To me love between us is not something that needs to be flaunted in public.

U: Good. All I wanted the people in this room to know was that prior to the meeting, words were exchanged. Marv, you expressed it admirably.

B: Yes, I agree.

Immediately after leaving the group Marv and I completed our conversation under private conditions.

B: I've noticed people tend to set up the same outline patterns and fall back into those past-life ruts. The next time you and I are thrown together to plan our coming lives, I'm hoping we're able to retain what we learned from this life and act more discerning. In this life we learned to hurt ourselves and each other. I don't want to repeat the pain I gave to you or myself. I'm assuming that on the other side we'll have other opportunities to express ourselves better.

Marv, what really made me a basket case was when I learned about the sorceress' life in which you were the beloved son. From her interpretation it tears me apart that you were poisoned and died a painful death because the sorceress was not able to save you. I suspect there is a lot of lingering guilt for her, thinking she had the skill to save you, but found she couldn't. The more I know about her life, the more I think she is key to the experiences I'm trying to work through now. She really seems to fit me like a glove. I even identify with some of her hang-ups that have stuck rather closely.

M: I don't know; I'm not privy to that yet. I've got an awful lot of stuff to undo from this life, so I'm afraid I've got to stick with this life, not previous ones. However, about my being your son, I have been told that's true; yet, that life didn't have much impact on me, because I died at such a young age with little memory of it. Nevertheless, I was the son you really wanted, so my death was very meaningful in your life. You put your hopes on me to save yourself and your kingdom as a son who would grow up to aid in your reigning capacity.

As we now know, I was not intended to live so that really crushed you. Being surrounded, you could see continuing would be hopeless. The best course would be for you and the girls to leave, so you plotted the course you took.

I've grown to understand your point of view. You did everything you could. You thought it through. You knew the girls were close to each other; they would always have each other once they were dead. You would be the person held responsible with the blight on your soul. You were willing, because you felt death was the best course of action. Therefore, you don't feel tainted like most of your contemporaries today. You retain that feeling. From my point of view, I understand your reasoning and don't find it shocking.

B: [*hesitates*] Is there anything else about that life that I need to know now?

M: It had a very great impact on you, because you're still working on the residue of it. I wanted to affirm your feeling; and I personally have come to understand your decision made back then. It's not that I approve in today's thoughts, but under the circumstances, it's understandable. If that's how you've resolved it, it's okay with me if you continue feeling okay about it in your mind.

B: Thank you, Marv. I appreciate your words. It's comforting to hear someone willing to empathize with my viewpoint from another era.

M: Is there anything else you want to know?

B: Can and do we meet when I'm sleeping? Is progress in healing our relationship possible then?

M: No. It has to be when you are awake because these are things we did while we were awake. Problems need to be solved in the same state we were in at the time.

B: Too bad. I was hoping we could make additional progress using my sleep time. However, this interesting tidbit will please you. During an energy healing session, Susan Gibson reached her arms above my prone body and appeared to begin pinching and striping an invisible cord. When finished, I asked her what that was all about.

Susan said that the thread is actually a relational cord. We have them with people in our lives. Cords don't go away after people die so the cord can be cleared and cleaned up of all the pain, leaving only the love. Sometimes the thread twists around a chakra and needs to be untangled. Generally, I do the work just on my client's side of the field, but Marv asked me, "Can you clean my side, too?" So I did.

Marv, I didn't know you were in attendance until after that appointment. As expected Samuel was silently observing and later asked me to thank Susan for the demonstration. The technique was new to him. Impressed, Samuel passed the technique on to others. So, the two of you taught my guides something they hadn't discovered yet. Surprisingly, the guides prefer the old-fashioned, personal recommendations over published medical books—despite the fact the other side is scientifically further advanced. Thanks for that bit of knowledge.

Speaking of the physical body, I am curious, Marv, being a physical educator, trainer, and athlete, is it tough not having the same kind of earthly body now?

M: No, I'm doing rather nicely without one. It's true, you don't have the maintenance; in my older age, I did start gaining a little weight. Being a skinny kid in my youth made me rude toward others facing weight problems. I think we all go through some kind of juvenile arrogance; I was certainly among the crowd in that one.

B: Again speaking of the physical body, would you be willing to let me know what your experience was like at the time of death and what you remember of your trip to the other side?

M: I'm afraid I was pretty typical of most people in my state those days. I was sick and under medication so I retained next to no images of the event. Frankly, some people on this side have expressed the opinion that they would like to see more people return to this side with their consciousness intact. The reason being the recently deceased would have a better understanding and appreciation of where they had been living and to where they are returning. It would be helpful.

B: Yes, I can see where that could help a person keep continuity in their life rather than leaving one location and waking up in a totally different environment. Just that would be a jarring adjustment.

M: Well, nice to chat with you. I don't want to tire you out, so I'll say goodbye for now.

❄ ❄ ❄

About a week later Beverly awoke to hear:

Beverly (B), Marvin (M)

M: Good morning, Beverly. I think you might want to know what I was researching this evening while you were sleeping. This is what I have discovered that should be of current interest to us. When I was very young, I was not able to see correctly. I had what was called Lazy Eye.

B: Yes, when we met, I was aware of your eye problem and the admiration your eye doctor had for your ability to play on the high school tennis team despite your focusing difficulties.

M: The reason for that eye problem was so I would not be able to look straight on at things the way a normal sighted person would see. In fact, I'll call my handicap a punishment for something in an earlier life that I carried over to this life. To me that was revolutionary news because you were the person who caused me to have this vision problem. One of the things that became my mission in this life was to overcome that visual problem and overcome my disdain for you for having been the cause of this affliction. I thought that was stunning news.

B: [*shocked and saddened*] Yeah. I agree, Marv. That's quite a revelation about a problem of yours to be dragged into this lifetime to be handled. It's amazing any of us can make any kind of progress knowing how much we load up ourselves with all kinds of handicaps from lives gone by—just like me.

What do you think? Is there more I need to know at this point? Or, what advice are you getting?

M: It's stunning and going to affect both of us back in time, not just this lifetime. I just thought you would be interested in knowing that and how that will be influencing our thoughts about each other and ourselves. That was just a "head's up" I wanted to send.

B: I appreciate being notified! We'll see what develops. Whew!

Disdain for me is harsh. I notice you didn't give me any details. But, this news is causing my sternum to feel uncomfortable. I better say thank you and stop the conversation at this point. I'm dumbfounded by what you're saying, but will wait for Samuel to spring the details on me at the optimum timing!

M: That was not my intention, but I agree. Goodbye for now and have a pleasant day.

※ ※ ※

Beverly (B), Samuel (Samuel)

At a later date I asked Samuel to expand on the information Marv had discovered:

B: Am I ready to know about Marv's eye problem in this lifetime to which I am somehow connected? Is that an appropriate topic for me to be thinking about?

Samuel: Probably you know all that's important. You were related, there is a connection between the two of you. It might ease your mind that he, in his outline, selected his punishment for his error. He was not assigned by God, whatever form you want to put that in, to earn penitence by living a lifetime with this visual handicap.

B: I had kinda worked that out in my own mind. He felt comfortable and satisfied enough with this challenge to live a decent, successful life—one that would be meritorious and satisfy any feeling of guilt he might have. I'm happy he wasn't so angry with himself that he built a hell!

Samuel: Yeah, that's pretty close to it.

B: That doesn't answer my part in it. I felt a little sick to my stomach when he told me he feels disdain, which slops over onto me. What's dangling over my head to be dealt with? What baggage is on my side of this equation?

At best, most of us give lip service to not being judgmental, but we really are. We always seem to be weighing ourselves and others on an invisible scale in our brain. I guess that's still true for me these days.

What surprises me during these talks with Marv, once I let off steam at my first encounter, I tapped into my deep well of love for him and his for me. Maybe there is something to the idea that life on Earth is a drama for us to try out other characters so we have a full range of acting experiences. We ask only spirits we really love to play the heavies in our performances because when we return to the other side and the masks are discarded, we can easily forgive and continue loving our protagonists.

The love I felt for Marv came from a deep well inside of me, not the shamefully giddy, silly daily emotions expressed like childish temper tantrums that I need to brush off my soul.

The next section of the book introduces you to another key person in my life, my brilliant sister Elaine who enjoyed an enviable flight home.

Part 4 Elaine

The 1966 Bride
Ballet Dancer
Patron of All Fine Arts
University of Michigan Graduate
Mechanical Engineer
Author's Sister

Elaine  Chapter 1

Elaine Hafemeister, *Engineer, Falk Corporation, a division of Sundstrand Corp.*, Published in *Spectrum*, Summer, 1978.

I was a serious engineering student at school, and worked my way through. Because I didn't expect to get married right away, I needed a real profession.

In the mid-fifties, times were very different. Some women with engineering degrees never did get a job in their field. A brilliant female student a year ahead of me at the University of Michigan ended up as a teaching assistant.

I interviewed at the place where I'd worked summers; they offered me a clerk technician job, but said they had no classification for women engineers! I remember signs saying, "Women need not apply" on college placement bulletin boards. In short, women were left with a terrible self-image. As odd as it sounds now, I was grateful to get hired in 1956 at Falk— as an engineering technician. It simply never occurred to me—or to a whole range of women—that I had the same rights as a man in getting a job as an engineer.

Nevertheless, I've liked working at Falk, and I enjoy the computer work I'm doing now. My job chiefly involves writing engineering programs that people in manufacturing, design and engineering use to do their work.

I like the people I work with, and that to me is important. The people at Falk are very supportive of each other. Also, a lot of your success depends on your boss; and I've had good bosses. From time to time, I've seen men who never let their female employees have a chance to progress. If you have a hopeless boss, I believe you're wasting your time working for him—or her.

Although I'm grateful to the women's movement for helping change some stereotyped ideas, in some ways it has encouraged some women to lose their feminine integrity. Too often I see women who are striving for success imitating some of the worst aspects of men. Instead of bringing grace and dignity to their jobs, they end up acting tough, which tends to overshadow their talents.

Another problem that the working woman faces today is finding a company that wants the woman for her individual talents rather than just a female to satisfy minority hiring requirements. This leaves women uneasy as to the motives of their employers.

I'm fairly easy-going about my profession. If someone doesn't recognize me as an engineer, I suggest they might prefer to talk with my supervisor. One person insisted on talking to my boss because he felt I couldn't possibly give him the correct information. The call involved a project that I had been more directly involved in that had my supervisor. As a result, I fed my boss the answers while he talked to the man on the phone.

Both men and women are changing. I think people today are more free. Not only can women hold responsible jobs, but a lot of men now can feel comfortable sharing the breadwinner role with their wives.

Elaine Hafemeister

Elaine  Chapter 2

The last time I saw my brother-in-law Larry and my sister Elaine both alive was September 3, 2017, their fifty-first wedding anniversary. I couldn't recognize Elaine as they sat at their group dining room table in their skilled nursing care residence.

It had been a long drive north from the Ohio River Valley to the Great Lakes. I was tired, but alarmed, when I saw my eighty-three year old sister practically skin and bones looking weak and lonely. In my mind she remained my bright, talented sister, three years my senior, who had been my role model of what an American girl should be: graceful, friendly, patient.

Dear Reader, for your clarity I am keeping events in chronological order as we move forward in time to the beginning of January 2018. While at home one evening, I was surprised to hear a voice in my head say, "I don't think I can take this much longer." I was alarmed. What's that all about? I couldn't figure it out so I tried to dismiss it.

The evening of January tenth I received two phone calls from the hospital in Milwaukee, the first to request that I sign papers to make medical decisions for my sister and the second to inform me my sister had just died. In real time for me, I knew next to nothing—other than being told she had died a few minutes ago.

Using my author's artistic license, I have combined two channeling sessions by Kym and me into one description of my sister's actual journey after her death. The following are Elaine's notated recollections of events that started a week before she died.

Beverly (B), Elaine (E), Kym (K), Elaine's Spirit Guide (SG), Samuel (S)

SG: Yes, the cry of anguish was just Elaine expressing her humanness. The reason she wasn't taken immediately was because she had been eager to leave before, then at the last moment, she changed her mind. When asked if she was sure, she said, "No, I'll stay a little longer for Larry." Elaine was checked multiple times by us to see if she was ready. Elaine is right here; let her have her say on this matter.

E: The nocturnal voice you heard at home in Cincinnati about "I can't take this much longer" was mine. I was getting desperate and didn't know how to get out. I was sending messages in hopes that someone would hear me. I was not particularly in pain, but I was very tired of feeling like an infant in such a helpless state, being ignored by people, and just being a commodity to be dealt with. Not being respected by other people is so debilitating!

Beverly, I would like to give you missing details as to what is happening in my life. First, I'm sorry we lived so far apart and were not able to visit more frequently. On your visits, I think you understood how really hopeless I was getting about my health and limited abilities. I could see in your eyes that you were concerned about what kind of treatment I was getting.

Some of the caregivers were tender and helpful. Others weren't paying attention to what they were doing. That's unfortunate because people in my condition, bedridden or in wheelchairs, are dependent on everything being supplied to them. But that's the unfortunate way we, as a society, have decided to handle our elderly, infirm people. I'm glad my outline went through these experiences, but I sure don't want to do it again!

When I grew weak, I was removed from my skilled nursing care residence of my retirement home and taken across the street to a Milwaukee hospital. When admitted, I was kept in a semi-coma state with unknown substances intravenously put into me for about a week. I had no choice in the matter; it was their procedure. At that stage I was in no position to argue, complain, or add my two cents. I had to go along with their agenda. When people sign a loved one or themselves over to hospice, I suggest they determine exactly what kind of treatment they are going to receive. All hospices are *not* alike. Some vary radically.

I don't believe I wished or requested that somebody come to rescue me in the hospital. By that I mean I was *not* frantically petitioning or praying to God to help me escape that life even though I had grown tired of living because I was cooped up in a body I couldn't control. I was absolutely fatigued and didn't want to continue living. I was glad to know there were people praying for me. The goal was to enable me to die rather quickly. I believe one of those people was you, Beverly, my only sibling. You were always sending me encouraging energy to be used in any way to my best advantage.

So, I want to acknowledge that, yes indeed, prayer is very important and helpful—particularly if you have a loved one who is frankly tired of living and would like to move on to their next experience. I want to encourage people who have that rapport with people to go ahead and pray, because it will help them as it did me. In my condition I was grateful.

B: I'm relieved to know my prayers were beneficial without being too opinionated about your needs. [*to Elaine's SG*] Along those lines of prayer, I heard an unknown, probably female voice say, more than once, "I don't think I can take this much longer." The speaker was getting frantic.

Meanwhile, I was trying to detect whose voice I was hearing. I wondered, "Why is she so desperate?" I'm embarrassed because once, a little snappy, I suggested, "Find your spirit guide." My real worry was that they may not have met. I never quite summoned up the courage to ask since I never was one to push my spiritual beliefs onto others.

When I figured out the voice was Elaine's, what should I have done? She was caught in a terrible spot, but why feeling desperate or abandoned?

SG: Don't worry; how you handled it was fine.

E: It's true that when my guide asked me, three separate times, whether I was ready to leave, I said yes but changed my mind. There were times when I was getting desperate and feeling lost. I made blanket statements out into, I thought, empty space, pleading for help. Then, my guide was right there to ask, "Are you sure this is the right time to go?"

My spirit guide presented other ideas to me that I could pursue if I wanted to stay in the body longer. I'm glad he did that since he was thinking of things I hadn't considered. He reasoned that if I got rid of my baggage on Earth, it would be well worth it in the future. Thus we worked together in that regard. He was always considering my best interest, so I'm grateful to him for his suggestions.

When asked again, I re-thought my statement and decided there were a couple more things I could do. So I deferred and said no. I did not really want to leave. That was my choice!

The timing of my leaving was an option I was given. It was entirely up to me. I don't know if that's true of other people, but in my case it was. I'm grateful because I have a nice sense of closure. I did everything I could think of to do; so I knew it was time for me to leave.

K: Beverly, let me paraphrase and summarize. You heard your sister's plea. The guides were waiting and they asked Elaine again, "Are you done?" She had been stretched to desperation three times. Each time she reversed her choice and stayed. This last time was different, because she said, "I've accomplished all I can."

B: I did not hear their conversation, but the last time I heard Elaine, I got a sensation of being surrounded by gold. It felt different; everything stopped. In that moment something had shifted.

E: Ideally the person who is nearing the end of their life would decide what was to be done medically for them before they were in that position. However, you can't always anticipate the needs you're going to have at that stage. It's important to do the best you can prior to that. Look at your own things, Beverly, and see if it's still how you want your Health Care Power of Attorney statement to read.

B: Listening to Terry Gross on NPR, I remember that one of her interviewees said, "Review that *Do Not Resuscitate* document *throughout* your lifetime. What you think you can't endure as a thirty year old may sound doable when you are fifty because you have found a productive way to live despite physical limitations."

If you don't have it in writing, you're saying the hospital decides what you need?

E: Yes. Sometimes hospitals administer painkillers way too early. To my surprise, I was lucky in that I didn't get those heavy drugs. I'm grateful and wish more people were able to do the same.

I've been told because my husband Larry wasn't deemed mentally competent to give his consent to drugs for me, the hospital turned to you, Beverly, as next of kin. By the time everything was legally completed, I had died, so hospice care was *never* officially given to me.

I discovered I died rather quickly while the hospital was preparing to send me back to my home in the skilled nursing care facility. I have since learned my friend the pastor had been alerted to that possibility by one of the nurses who said, "Whatever you do, don't let them send Elaine back to her residence because it is so exhausting when that happens. It drags things out. Better to leave her in the hospital hospice unit." I had almost used up my allotted hospice time, so they wanted to move me back home. Thus, dying quickly helped me a great deal.

Not having received much in the way of drugs while in the hospital allowed me to be alert when I crossed over. I was grateful to be aware during the whole transition process. I'm also grateful for the opportunity to talk with you, Beverly, while I'm in this transitional stage.

Let me tell you what I actually experienced when I was ready to die in the hospital. In the moments before my death, I was surrounded by lots of spirits. I recognized some of them, but some were complete strangers. I felt very comfortable and unafraid because I felt I was, and would be, in good hands during this whole experience.

At the moment of death, I was immediately plucked out of my body. Plucked is the correct word because it was a gentle reaching down, a gentle pull, and out my head I went, leaving my body behind. I don't know how I was plucked out but indeed I was. I felt no pain or sentimental fondness for my body. By then I was annoyed with my body because it failed me in the last several years. I left my body without regrets.

When I did separate from my body, I was not alarmed. I knew it was happening. I knew what was going on although I had no recollection of having died before. There was nothing frightening or particularly abnormal feeling. I guess I recognized it as the next stage. This is how you get there. "Just sit tight and let mother nature take its course," were my thoughts.

I would like people to know if they can find that serenity in themselves, it will be a great comfort. At least it was for me. I was very much at ease throughout the whole event; the whole process was—I guess I'll use the word—pleasant. I hope that will eliminate the fear for some people and the dread on the part of loved ones who are left behind. While a source of grief, it is to be remembered that it's a natural process. In the long run, death may be the best thing for many people. So, do not get all worked up about something that is a natural process.

I was completely dependent on those who supported me during that process. Immediately I could see we were going towards the ceiling, out through the ceiling, and out into the dark night into the dark sky. Again, I still had no fear and was comfortable with the process. Is that clear?

B: Yes, I can visualize that without a problem. Was that when your spirit guide became visible to you?

E: No. I didn't see my spirit guide until I was away from the Earth itself. I was happy to see him because by that time I had become quite accustomed to his visiting me as a voice in my head.

B: Good. Any other description of that period? Did you have a sense you were being pulled away from the Earth's atmosphere?

E: Yes, having been a student of geography, I could see various parts of the world that I recognized. I could identify some of the continents and knew I was leaving the area. Again, I still had no fear and was comfortable.

You made the comment the other day that warriors were accustomed to traveling in the astral plane. That's probably true for warriors who do the kind of work that you do. But because of my kind of work, a warrior-grounder hybrid, I was much more Earth-based. So I want to clarify, I don't know if I did any more astral traveling than the average, normal person. It was not something I was quite familiar with, but I was not feeling fearful. It was a big event!

B: Good. How did you know where to go? Was your spirit guide in the lead?

E: I knew not how to get here and still don't. I was escorted by people who knew where I needed to go. I have no idea how long the trip took nor where I am now. I don't know what to call it—a planet or what. I'll call it "home" as many frequently do.

Yes, my guide was right up there in the front as was I. It was a marvelous trip. I was out of my body but still felt body parts tingling in my arms and legs that hadn't been awakened in years. I was starting to feel wonderful already. As we approached this home area, everything was extremely familiar to me. I knew I had lived happily here before.

Somebody must wire ahead. People knew a party was about to start because as we arrived, there was a congregation of folks who were expecting me. So, I was even happier to speed up because I was overjoyed to see these people again. Some were friends from "home" and others were friends who had departed the Earth level earlier, so we could all renew acquaintances again.

The area was loaded with friends and family. I was pleased and felt so loved by all the people. I had no idea how many people would remember me and care about me. I'm so grateful for their reception; and those people are still with me. It's wonderful! Still, I was very much in my comfort zone.

B: Well, Elaine, how shall I say it? You've had so many years of being inhibited in a wheelchair. After your ordeal I'm sure everyone wanted you to feel at home as quickly as possible. I'm pleased at your reception. I'm happy for you and how this has all worked out. I hope you know by now your spirit guide is extremely proud of you, as are all of us.

It sounds like in your case you were not fatigued after your trip, but filled with engendered energy.

E: Yes, very much so; and I want to thank the people who were praying for me right along. Some were strangers and some were people who I knew. I guess I didn't give prayer enough thought while I was alive. I had put it in the myth department of life and not a serious way to help. Instead, you can contribute to the health of people and the planet even when staying in your own house and generating good energy thought patterns that the world is craving at this time!

Beverly, I'm wholeheartedly in favor of taking advantage of any opportunity of communication between us. I see you are, too, because I see the two of us vibrating together.

B: You've got a lot to teach me! I look forward to it.

K: [*to Beverly*] It's a great gift to be connected to Elaine, to see her process, and to record it. It is important for our readers to understand what you did to help Elaine in the early phases of crossing over. She wants to share a bunch of things with her sister.

B: I don't know what I did. I mentally sent information to two of her girl friends as I was getting Elaine ready to cross over in a dance costume worn in her youth. I actually felt I was helping her get dressed just as I physically did late in life when we were together on our Road Scholar[1] vacations. Was that a dream or close to what actually happened? It felt real, but I don't know how to put that in perspective.

E: [*chuckles*] I have to comment about how you dressed me, Beverly. Yes, I'm told it was a rather novel way for you to prepare me and pick what I was to wear for the trip. Then for you to escort me part way and abruptly look over your right shoulder and return back to Earth was unusual. I assumed you were called back. I had kinda zoomed on ahead. I was not trying to be rude; I was just excited and eager to get here.

B: Actually, I felt you were being well-escorted because I could see many colored lights in the distance and sensed my part was over—time for me to go back to my bed.

E: Definitely. There were a lot of souls around me, showing me the way. I had no concerns about that. But, I didn't want you to feel I was ungrateful. So here is my heartfelt thank you.

B: Truth of the matter is, Elaine, I don't think I would have been allowed to go much further, even though as a warrior I'm more accustomed than the average person to doing astral traveling. I never assumed I'd be able to go very far. It wasn't my time, as they say.

E: The party began before I even landed! When people saw me decked out in my gypsy dancing costume with ballet slippers and tambourine, they hooted with laughter and glee. Instantly everybody put on party clothes. I want to thank you or your guides, whoever thought that up. That was such a wonderful entrance for me to know that this is the beginning of the fun times again. Thank you.

B: I have to say I kept seeing that photograph of the teenaged you in your dance costume for several days while you were in

---

1 Formerly known as Elderhostel.

the hospital. The picture would pop in my mind for absolutely no reason. So, when it was time for you to leave, there was no question as to what dress you should wear. I'm so pleased. I was hoping your outfit would add to the festivity of your return.

I thank Samuel and the crowd who hang around me. They have their own weird sense of humor like you and I do, Elaine.

E: I thank them for such a joyous trip.

B: Now I'd like to see if you can give me a few more details about the trip. Did you feel like you were being carried there? Or were you propelling yourself? Or like birds do when they migrate, did you sense a built-in, magnetic, flight path to your destination?

E: I don't know how much I was doing and how much was joyful anticipation in knowing where I was going. I wasn't paying that much attention to the mode. [*chuckle*] I failed here as a scientist.

B: Don't worry. We will accept your lapse. So you were immediately greeted with a party; and since then, I gather, there have been non-stop parties going on. Right?

E: Yes, there are plenty of parties.

What I have omitted telling you so far is the fact that when I arrived here, I could see there were many people from many stages of my life. When I say stages, that's the hard part to describe. You and Kym have been working on understanding the concept of your multiple lives and how you're living them all at the same time. So, maybe you can catch on to what I'm picturing for you here.

It is true. We are living several lives at a time. It's so alien to us that it will be hard to convey how it works. On the Earth level, I'd say 99.9% of us are completely oblivious to that fact. When you and I talk about multiple lives, there needs be some frame of reference for people to glom onto and work it through as best they can.

Even though there will be a lot of frustrated people who can't visualize something that complex, this is part of the life they are already living. So it may help them to start thinking of their life in a more complex pattern than previously envisioned. For many this concept will have to be trickled down with advanced knowledge.

The first thing I recognized when I came back here was the fact that I did have these multiple lives going on at the same time. Some of my "Elaine" lives are still living on Earth and some are living here. I am able to be in contact with them because of my current level.

B: Yes, our mother has talked about having that same ability while being three levels ahead of me.

E: That's true. In mother's case she is very much aware of her other lives and is comfortable with the fact that she can, in a sense, stand aside and watch what's going on with these other lives. How are they dealing with the same basic problem that she experienced when in the body? How do they feel about it because of their current age in that particular life? It's fascinating for her.

As I mentioned, when I arrived I was granted the same ability to know I was in various forms both on this side and on Earth. I have no idea what level I'm on, but I have that advantage. I don't want to say it complicates my life; it just doesn't shake me up.

It's interesting. I have a more distant feeling about myself as Elaine and my other lives by observing, almost like a movie or play. These are just characters on a stage I'm watching although I know they are me. I know that some people who are key in their lives are also key in mine.

That's one way our lives get interwoven. As I've heard you and Kym say, it is absolutely mind-boggling how all of that gets sorted out, organized, and yet makes sense. It's a very efficient way of learning. It's complicated, but on the other hand, it's wonderful to be able to observe this. So that's a heads-up to you of what, like mother, I've been learning.

B: The sprinkling of the same key figures in multiple lives probably makes for serious progress for those people once they understand how they are able to help each other. No wonder it probably feels good to take a party break every now and then.

E: Yes, but life is calming down. Many people have gone back to their normal activities. As expected, the closer the relationship, the longer people stay at parties. I'm assuming we will soon put away our party costumes and dig into whatever conversations of a serious nature have to be talked about. Even you and I can talk again later ...

❊ ❊ ❊

Beverly (B), Elaine (E), Samuel (S)

On a later day was this conversation:

E: Reflecting back on what I think about my recent life, I'm glad now I had my Elaine life experience, but it was not at all fun! The fact that my physical disabilities went on many years was extremely wearing on me. I am glad now to be entering another phase of my life. For that reason I'm grateful you were able to help me a little in getting away from Earth.

B: FYI, near the end as you grew sicker, I was working with Larry's guide, Al, in hopes of being helpful. As you know, partially deaf, Larry could not hear you, and you could only whisper due to your illness. I planted the seed for you two to communicate telepathically.

I asked my spirit guide this question:

Samuel, was that a good, useful idea? Was that true or just a hope? I don't want to suggest things to people if it has no merit.

S: That was good. You started problem solving. You could also have said, "Either turn up the volume on your (non-existent) hearing aid, Larry, or on your (non-existent) microphone, Elaine." You helped them problem solve and be creative. So, yes, it did have merit. Readers should know that they, too, can help others in the same way. It works. Even when alive, yet sleeping, any person can create this type of connection.

❈ ❈ ❈

After a steady diet of celebratory parties, the next chapter will follow Elaine as she releases her pent up need to move with grace and expression after years of physical limitations.

Furthermore, those holding council seats on the other side take the opportunity to hear a current view of earthly conditions from one freshly returned.

Elaine  Chapter 3

Guessing what was in my sister's best interest after her death, I decided to leave her alone—hopefully with family and friends—on the other side for almost a week after her life-altering change on January 10, 2018. At that stage I was unaware of her experiences as told to you readers by Elaine herself in Chapter 2. So, I figured whenever Elaine was ready and wanted to contact me, it would be best for her to decide.

However, speaking telepathically to various people, their opinion was I was in error. So after her death, my recorded channeling sessions began. With the help of others, for the first time since she died, I got Elaine "live" on the line while I sat alone in my bedroom on Tuesday evening, the sixteenth. The following is a continuation of Elaine's events. Believe me, that felt overwhelming when I realized now I wasn't connected to Area Code 414 Wisconsin. I had just dialed my sister's new secret area code—number unknown—somewhere in space! WOW.

Beverly (B), Elaine (E)

B: Is it true, Elaine, you're there?

E: Yes, I'm here ready, willing, and able to talk to you. I'm surrounded by a lot of people, most of whom I know and recognize from the early part of my Elaine life and have been enjoying a reunion with all of them. It's absolutely wonderful to spend time with them, and frankly, to be able to talk and move around whenever I feel like it. I no longer depend on a wheelchair as I was in the latter part of my physical life. Indeed, it was a long time, but being physically restricted was what I had agreed to do.

B: I'm thrilled that you're doing so well. I'm assuming you've seen our parents.

E: Yes, I've been overjoyed to see both of them and how they have matured. Now I've been able to catch up with what their lives have been like. So much was hidden from us. In Mother's case we had no idea what she was coping with in her inner life[2]. I hold her in high regard just as you do, particularly for what she has undertaken and undergone. I know you've been enjoying them from your distance; and that's one of the great joys we both have now.

❋ ❋ ❋

Later in the week, Beverly invites Kym into the living room to channel Elaine and her spirit guide. To intertwine the energy of the sisters for a stronger reading, Kym asks Beverly to say both names. This is what resulted:

Beverly (B), Elaine (E), Kym (K), Samuel (S), Toby (T), and U (Unknown voice)

K: There's a humorous energy in the room filled with a bunch of people. One large jovial man in particular is prominent. As soon as I asked to hear all their names, he put his hands together and lowered his head in mock prayer. He was being comical about the seriousness of you sisters. Mister, who are you?

U: A dear friend.

K: To whom? Beverly or Elaine?

---

2   Unaware as Mother was of her role as a warrior, and seeing or hearing frightful things with her physical senses and mind, she became stressed to the breaking point and killed herself to stop the visions. Details are in *We Got It All Wrong*, Book 1 and Book 2

U: Elaine.

K: He reminds me of a slimmer John Goodwin who played nice guy, Dan Conner, on TV's "Roseanne".

B: Is that Elaine's guide?

K: Might be.

[*to the man*] Do you want to give me your name?

T: [*telepathically received*] Toby.

K: [*to Bev*] Wonderful. Elaine is having fun on pointe shoes, dancing around the studio as a young girl of about thirteen years. I sense other people are here, but I really don't see them. Elaine and Toby are much clearer to me. Elaine, completely ignoring us, is still dancing circles around Toby.

T: I know you've come to figure out what Elaine is up to now. She's up to just being Elaine immersed in feeling good, feeling alive. We're helping her to heal and feel back in control. She has a lot of repercussions from the life she chose to have. We're in the process of helping her to re-engage in herself, her joys, and lack of responsibilities. Her illness carried a lot of responsibilities. Elaine's been the trooper freed from that obligation.

K: What responsibility was she carrying by having this illness?

T: Do you want to go into that heavy topic now?

K: It's information to us. I have no agenda.

B: Well, I have an agenda! Elaine knew about outlines when we first talked on January 16th after she crossed over. Is there something written in our outlines that is to be addressed during this transition time? In other words, when Elaine settles down from dancing, is there something ...

T: Time for that later. Never fear, Elaine is going to be involved in helping you learn more—you personally and us as a group. She's just in a rejuvenation period now.

B: She's welcome to her R and R!

K: Bev wants her to have fun and not push her; but when she wants to focus on this, let Bev know.

[*to Bev*] Elaine has a good guide because Toby values fun, too.

T: She was an adult for too long in this life. She had a great life because she accomplished so much of what she wanted to achieve. But she's in the midst of taking off that costume—that suit of adulthood.

E: [*talking over her shoulder as she continued dancing around Toby*] Bev, be sure to journal your experiences with me, because you're emotionally connected, and I died so recently. You've not had fresh transition input from our mother, uncle, or dad since they died so long ago.

B: I was surprised, Elaine, you died first after the earlier conversations with Larry's spirit guide[3]. I must say, I'm not unhappy.

E: You would have handled it either way, but it's better for me to be out of the mess of tying up so many loose ends. Toby said it was my choice and my timing. I haven't regretted it a bit. What Toby is not saying is my husband will not be staying long on Earth. Larry hasn't, yet, worked past his hanging-on-for-dear-life attitude, but he's real close. I stayed long enough so he could work through stuff.

B: Three cheers for you, Elaine. I congratulate you. You've been a gem!

E: Larry was my reason to stay until I knew he would be okay.

B: It sounds like, in the future, Elaine and I have something that can and needs to be written. Is there something in the Hafemeister girls' outlines that needs to be done at this time?

T: You're definitely going to be working together. That's why she's doing her process right now. That does not mean she cannot work with you at the same time.

---

3 See Larry, Part 5, Chapter 1

K: [*being a distance from the dancing child*] Toby, can Elaine stop dancing to talk to us?

[*to Beverly*] Toby told me to ask her.

[*to Elaine*] Elaine, your sister wants a few minutes of your time then you can go back to your pirouettes.

[*to Bev*] Elaine's wearing a pink tutu and her hair is pulled up into something pink in her hair. She's stopping and sitting down.

E: How can I help?

B: I'm glad you're able to enjoy dancing again.

E: It has been one party after another party.

K: Beverly wants to talk to you about what you know.

E: I've gone back to infancy to relive my babyhood with Mother and Dad before you were born. As young parents sitting on the floor in front of a fireplace, they played with me, expressing their love for me as their first child while I lie on my back on the floor.

B: Remember, Kym, my mother told us she was soothing infants in hospitals on the other side.[4] Playing with Elaine could be a personal extension of that exercise. As a colicky baby, Elaine might have had a rough start and this was a way to redo or heal. Smart move.

K: So, you have the option to re-live situations when you have just transitioned out of a life. In our world that's a lot of years for Elaine—eighty plus Earth years. Everyone has the option to go back and re-experience events from a new point of view. Elaine took the opportunity to re-experience it in all its glory, which she didn't at the time. It's part of the healing process, the review process, and the understanding of why we are the way we are.

B: I'm really pleased. Here you've got a girl in the 1950s who's

---

4   See *We Got It All Wrong*, Book One

on the path to becoming an engineer. Being a woman she wasn't going to be welcomed with opened arms into that profession. Starting off being appreciated by her parents in childhood is important for a solid foundation of her self image, when later on she's going to see a lot of snubbing from her profession.

E: In my life review, I saw I didn't bite on to rejection, but it spurred me on in many ways. You're coming from your Beverly sensitivity. I didn't have your Beverly sensitivity. It was hard; I'm not saying it wasn't, but that's what spurred me on. I wanted to do what I wanted to do. The adversity in the male occupation, the adversity as a woman getting a higher education, the adversity of marrying the man I did, all those were purposely picked by me to spur me on.

B: It's almost "I'll show you."

E: No, you're wrong. I don't feel any of the anger that is usually attached to "I'll show you." Bev, you have the underlying anger. You've got the "I'm the boss of me" attitude.

K: I sense a difference. Elaine didn't need to tap into anger to be motivated. Challenges made her want to be more. It was a huge motivator for her.

B: Yeah. That fits, doesn't it! My guess, as Beverly, was off target and too timid; the other was too aggressive, which Elaine never would be. Yet, she was going to do life her way.

K: She was a strong woman, but she didn't have to be a loud woman to be a strong woman. She was a quiet woman. Her husband spurred her on. Her career spurred her on. You tend to see her life all from your point of view, which is just not true. It's a disservice to you to look constantly at her life through your lens.

B: It's true and it's a disservice to Elaine and Larry. Yeah, I would probably be totally miserable in her life saddled with my baggage. She was not.

K: There were times when it was very hard and a big struggle, but her intelligent husband kept her on her toes and grounded in herself. Yet, he was not an easy man.

E: But Larry brought me the strength I needed. He was a perfect match for me; and he loved me.

K: [*to Beverly*] I feel all this love for her husband. She didn't want to do it without him. Larry was strong in a way that was different than her way.

E: Bev and I were not raised to show our affection.

B: Generally that northern German personality was not demonstrative, but Larry was affectionate toward Elaine until illness caused stress.

E: I don't regret my life. I don't regret my life with Larry, I don't regret the path that I chose. I don't regret any single bit. But enough of that.

K: [*to Bev*] Elaine just jumped up and started dancing again.

T: There will be time, Beverly.

B: But this is not the time.

T: This is the time. She can do more than one thing at a time. If you need her and desire to work with her, you can.

B: Let me see what Samuel says. Was there something she and I were hoping to do? Is this the time?

S: This is all for a reason, Bev. Communicate with her. Talk. Journal. You need this and she needs to be with you. It will not stop her from dancing around the room like a young girl. That's where she is now, but she's also a mature Elaine who wants to have conversations with her sister.

B: Is there an end goal in sight? Or do I just write it all down and worry about it later?

S: Worry about it later. Just write it all down. It will become clear to you what this is all about. Right now it's about you spending time with your sister and healing you of missing your sister. Write and record everything you have. It's a healing period for you, too.

K: Don't overthink this. Just spend the time together and learn all the things you're desperately needing to know before Larry gets there.

B: Yes, he will be a force to be reckoned with once he gets back with Elaine.

K: All three spirit guides gave a thumbs up sign. Elaine's twirling again.

E: I'm hoping we will be able to continue with these conversations even after I've adjusted back to my place on this side of the veil, as you call it. I'm hopeful we can establish greater rapport because I think we have a lot to tell and teach each other.

B: Yes, I hold you in high regard and look forward to these conversations.

❄ ❄ ❄

A few days later:

Beverly (B), Elaine (E)

B: Tell me what happened after the party fun slowed down.

E: I was taken to a panel of people in authority positions. They were the governing, administrative type people who welcomed me back home and were anxious to debrief me on what my experiences had been on Earth—just the day-to-day basic issues that people like me in Wisconsin experienced, including our frustrations, our stresses and physical conditions in terms of food, water, and environmental conditions.

I was quite impressed by the kinds of questions they asked, their depth, and seriousness. They wanted to get as good a picture as possible about what life in America was like for a person in my particular stage or position. I'm assuming they do that for every person who arrives.

B: Are you suggesting they are worried about what we are doing to the planet? That's how I interpret those kinds of questions.

E: Yeah, I think they were. Polar bears are coming into my mind. I think they were not only concerned about our lives but the whole life of the planet. In some regard I found that refreshing but also stressing. It was something on my mind; and I'm glad they were attuned to the personal views of a newly arrived woman. It gave me confidence to see that they were concerned with those kinds of questions. I was happy to know that about the people who I will say "are in charge" of watching the impact humans have on the universe, more than just Earth. That was gratifying.

Of course, the scholars here are much further advanced scientifically than those on Earth. Elementary information about the laws of nature are studied here and minimal knowledge trickles down from here to Earth. I think you understood that years ago when you talked to Herb who, even though he was a physicist, felt impressed and overwhelmed like a child in kindergarten with what he didn't know while on Earth. The scientists here know so much more than us. That would be my same appraisal of the knowledgeable folks on the panel I appeared before.

Are there other questions?

B: After debriefing, were you pretty much on your own to determine what you wanted to do with your time, if there is time? [*laughing*] Did you have any other obligations or requirements?

E: I enjoyed making choices because it had been so long since I could implement them. This was a wonderful chance to get back in the swing of being responsible for myself in terms of what I do and how I entertain myself. To exercise my free will without having to ask someone to help me or please provide something I needed. This has been glorious for me to get back to being an independent person!

I have not felt any pressure to join any club, do some work, or sign up for some committee. But, I'm at liberty as a free agent. Asking myself what needs my attention now, I have been tempted to make commitments, but I've kept them to the minimum. As you can imagine, if you go on a long vacation to another continent on Earth, once you get home you need a little time to catch up and see how things have changed.

In other words, when I look at my neighborhood, it's the same house. Many of my same neighbors are here, but I can sense some things have been added and some things subtracted. It's just a matter of catching on to where I was and what I would like to do in the future. I have decided not to rush. I'm pleased to have this kind of luxury. I'm assuming other people are in that same position.

B: That makes me wonder since you have been described as a hybrid[5] of a warrior and a grounder, are there work-related clubs? Are you automatically members of those two groups? Are you free to hop to some other group if you want?

E: I think I will stay where I am doing a little of both. When trapped in my wheelchair, I thoroughly enjoyed having little kids come to me telepathically so I could teach them and help them work out their problems. It saved me from going nuts; and I think I helped them. It was a win-win for both of us.

I was glad I had the grounder personality and also the ability of the warriors to reach out and help people who are on the edge of facing crises or decisions. Working to have a positive impact on them, I'm happy to remain this hybrid here just as I was on Earth side—but without the wheelchair.

B: I would guess these work related people meet together because they share common interests. I'm assuming you have been able to do that and perhaps as a recent returnee they want to know what you have been doing.

E: Oh yeah! [*chuckles*] I've been invited to be guest speaker. No doubt I will do that. It will bring them up to date in

---

5   See glossary to see how hybrid is defined on Earth. On the other side, hybrid has a slightly different meaning but unknown to the author at this time.

terms of how I was experiencing my life. Many will find that interesting and kinda fun for me to review my lifetime. Of course, I didn't know consciously I was working with children. Whereas Mother knew something odd was going on in her life, but didn't know she was a warrior—a job description that was not in her vocabulary. Then you, in the later part of your life, also discovered you were in that group of people who helps folks needing to be rescued from hell.

Unaware in life that I was able to help others, I will be interested to see how many other people in the group had a similar life of doing the work without knowing it. Or, did many of them retain the information during their life that they belonged to this group and that was their mission? I was like you, struggling with being a part of a group and not knowing this was something I had signed up to do before being born. I will be able to inquire about that kind of thing, too. Counting the show of hands should be fascinating.

Is there anything else you would like to know?

B: When did you and Toby consciously meet up?

E: Well, I knew him on this side, but growing up I did not know anything about spirit guides. As you recall our Methodist church did not talk about such things, so it was never in my view of life any more than it was yours. It was something that never occurred to me. So it was a complete surprise when he appeared to me and introduced himself.

B: Because he saw he was consciously needed by you?

E: Yes, I would say that. He was carefully monitoring my experiences and how I was doing. I think he just felt this was the time to step forward and let me know he was always at my side even though I couldn't necessarily see him.

B: Do you recall what age you were when this happened?

E: I'm not sure, but it was certainly later—in the last few years.

B: This is where my embarrassment lies. In your later years, I regret I couldn't find the right words to be more informative to you on this topic, so I'm glad Toby took matters in his own hands and didn't let you feel like you were dangling alone.

E: That's true.

B: Do you see much of Toby now that you're on the other side?

E: Oh, yes. We work constantly together. He is my main man! I'm grateful he's such a perceptive, kind, and funny person. It's a joy to be with him and get his insights. I feel very lucky to have him as my spirit guide.

B: Good. One last question: my small book discussion group has said they will be interested to hear and critique my notes surrounding your transition. Is sharing okay or would you rather I not?

E: I think that would be fine. I would be interested in knowing how that works out for them. In your little group of older people, I think that would be helpful for them. Yes, as far as I'm concerned, you can go ahead and plan that. I'll ask folks on this side and see what happens.

❋ ❋ ❋

After an interim of time, Beverly got this news:

Beverly (B), Elaine (E), Toby (T)

E: I am happy to report that all systems are "go ahead" here. We have been granted permission to pursue our conversations about this transition of mine to the other side. There had been some objections and concerns that maybe we were moving along too fast for Earth to understand. When reviewing the situation, it was determined in some sense your society's beliefs have been lagging behind our reality. Lack of growth on Earth has not helped us work on our mutual problems. Ignorance is prohibiting us from being realistic about our expectations of both sides.

Be careful to whom you give this information at this stage.

It's going to take a while to get it in a workable form as a booklet, whatever you and I can manage. It's important that it be a balanced report.

When the time comes, we will be closely scrutinized. Editors will be brought on board to be sure we get a nice balance to inform people of the process. Also, we'll explain what's expected of them and what they're expected to do on this side of life so they don't have any false illusions.

You're thinking there is some kind of a liaison person through which we are to work. Yes, there will be a person assigned to steer us and also work with our spirit guides. We will all be in collaboration with each other and hope things will run smoothly and efficiently. We will try to make as few false steps as possible.

Thank you for sending the thoughts and concerns you've had. I think it was helpful for them to see there are people on Earth who are wanting this to be a success. In some regards I think people on Earth would be relieved to know that so much good stuff is happening on this side. I think they would draw hope from the future of, in our case, the Earth, which a lot of us are so concerned about.

B: Good! Would some other person in the room want to add something?

T: Wish us well and know we are supporting you. However, people on your side do not fully understand how important it is to include Source in their decisions. Pray for wisdom on all sides. Source will give us some guidance here.

We are much further away from God than people on Earth think. They assume this is heaven, but it is not. It's important for people to understand this is one of the next levels. Even some who are here don't really grasp that knowledge. We're still part of an illusion, just a slightly different illusion than we had on Earth. And the journey goes on. The struggle will be worked out. We don't want Elaine to fret because we love her brave, direct, let's-talk-about-it attitude.

B: Let me ask you this question. Your community, are you all on the same level? Or are there several levels living together?

E: Actually, it's like Earth in that it's a mix of people. Some are, I hate to use the word "slower," but I must. They haven't developed their awareness as much as other people have.

B: Does that cause friction?

E: Everybody seems to get along. Because people have gone through stages, I don't find them condescending. It's more a matter of empathy and a feeling of patience that so and so is at this stage. That's okay, they are working on it. They will move up once they make some connections and gain understanding. So, for myself, I haven't felt embarrassed or frustrated at any unkindness said or thought about people. That's one of the joyous aspects. It's hard to explain but certainly helps set the tone here. It's truly more of a harmonious environment than on Earth. That's partly why I thought fondly of this place and recognized it as I was returning here.

B: But I gather on that side you are able to eliminate that really harsh edge we seem to hang on to at the Earth level.

E: Yes, we are not bombarded by that nastiness so common on Earth. Frankly, that's why people don't want to go back to Earth. Therein lies a problem. Unless people go back, we can't progress as a group. Sometimes people who have not returned in a while get a little pressure put on them. I don't know whether that's good or bad because sometimes they have valid reasons for not going back and are worried they can't handle what they might have to face. So I can understand their apprehension.

Maybe that's an area that needs looking into. I would hope people would know what they are going to face and have some schools of preparation on this side that would carry over into the actual trip into Earth.

B: That strikes me the same way. For example, if I were trained to become a warrior, I would hope to be trained into dealing with everyday living problems, too. Maybe some people will have ideas on how they could contribute. It's gotta be a shock to go from where you are living to becoming an Earth baby learning from scratch from parents who don't remember why they are there. Quite a challenge! Anything to ease that abrupt change would help.

E: Well when you get here you can start that conversation. [*laughter*]

B: Right! [*laughter*] That would be a good thing.

E: I'm aware that you are now gradually being introduced to the idea that we have disagreements, which is totally different from what you were taught in your first conversations with Kym. I'm afraid it was her veil you were seeing through, which wanted the other side to be more harmonious than what goes on behind the scenes. So, you won't be surprised to hear this, but it has been hard for her to accept that we are not all thinking alike. It is more a wish on her part because in her early life there was little harmony. You have to give her some leeway to her viewpoint, but this is my viewpoint of what's happening with her.

Here, we are not allowed, or cannot seem to have, the ability to take out any kind of deep angst on each other. It is a wonderful atmosphere to be able to express your opinion fully and other people know where you stand and that's okay. No reason to fight on this level. That's why people don't want to leave.

B: I'm curious. You've met my team. So if you and I continue working together, we will continue to run into each other and be more interwoven.

E: Yes, I say that is true; and I think you're concerned about Samuel.

B: [*surprised and bewildered*] Yes, I really am, but I don't know why. I'm hoping he's okay.

E: Don't worry, Beverly. He's a great supporter of yours and sometimes he says things that ... you'd have to be here to understand. I suspect you do a little bit. I don't want you to have any doubts about him. He's very much a supporter of you as I try to be of him.

I'm aware it's the responsibility of your spirit guide Samuel to keep things on track, so I will always check with him. You have the reputation of insisting that people go through him, so I will follow that lead.

B: Perfect. I get frustrated because I'm still not doing well about my failures concerning (1) protecting myself from unwanted spirits and (2) discernment. It's my own negligence that gets me in trouble. Having confessed that, I think I will depart for this evening. I hope tomorrow we'll be free to have another chat. Thank you so much, Elaine. Bye now.

S: Goodbye, Beverly.

E: Note: that farewell was said by Samuel. He was practically in tears by your love and concern for him.

B: He's such a sweetheart. I'm curious. When I'm in the Tender Beverly personality, does he get stuck with a Tender Samuel persona? Does he have to put on what I am?

E: No, that's the real him. He's a softy.

B: Good, that's why I'm so fond of him. I don't think being sensitive is a flaw.

E: Nor does he.

B: That's good. We're okay together. *(Remembering my soulmate Herb was the same way, too.)* My regards to Toby, too!

❄ ❄ ❄

The next assignment on our agenda was to acknowledge officially the physical departure of Elaine from the Milwaukee scene. Despite her dread, the day taught us all some wonderful, even profound lessons.

Elaine  Chapter 4

April 28, 2018

As planned, I started the day contacting Elaine since it had been so long since I felt her presence. I could feel the gathering of people who had come to offer their energy, so we had a good connection. I don't know specifically who they are, but I don't sense they came to talk, just add energy. They sensed my nervousness and wondered why. I don't know why, but that's how I always feel.

Beverly (B), Elaine (E), Samuel (S)

B: I am calling today to wish Elaine a happy what would be her 84th birthday. Is she there and able to talk to me?

E: Yes, I am here with many, many of our friends, people that we both know, who are here to aid in this conversation. We sense your apprehension and frankly are puzzled by it. I guess you're just busy being Beverly. You are always tense. We wish you weren't, but this is the role you are playing out now, so we understand it.

Thank you for remembering me on my birthday. I've been very busy; and I haven't gotten back to you, so I don't know what's been going on with you. I hope we can use this time to catch up with each other.

First, let's talk about the planned memorial service for me

on May 6 and get it out of the way because it's on your mind, too. Yes, it's true, I really didn't want such an event to take place because memorials always sound so sentimental. However, I've come to the realization that actually a lot of it is for the benefit of those living. I don't expect many people to attend because, frankly, most of them are on this side. We communicate very nicely and get together whenever we wish. My main concern is for those people who have not yet had that connection. Even you have not properly grieved. I see you are now beginning to realize you haven't sat down and thought about losing what we are both losing.

B: [*tearfully*] I'm aware now. For sure, a chapter in both of our metaphysical books has closed.

E: And speaking of books, our baby books might give you some interesting tidbits for your part of the service. Mother did a wonderful job of keeping notes on our life as kids. There might be an entertaining event to relay, but remember your purpose is to help people who attend find a way to grieve in a healthy way. If you can do both, I will be happy.

Telling people you have conversed with me on the other side doesn't matter to me. What matters is their health, their ability to adjust, to find peace, and to be more receptive when it comes time for them to leave and join me on this side. If you keep that in mind, I would be appreciative.

As far as Larry goes, I have been trying to get in contact with him. As you know he is a stubborn and determined person who sticks with things as he sees them. He's not particularly open-minded to new ideas. In my outline on this side, I agreed to marry him, knowing it was going to be a bit of a challenge for him to loosen up to new ideas. He was going to be very regimented in how he thought about things and as inflexible in life as he was nimble in his mechanical engineering skills. That was one of my challenges; and I'm still working on it and still trying to help him become more flexible.

I hear you praying for both of us and our ability to accomplish things. I encourage that; I appreciate that because that gives us that little bit of extra oomph. [*chuckles*] Larry is a bit of a tough case. I expect that once he is acclimated to life on the other side, I will have plenty of time to work on these things and see if we can loosen him up. Since your guide Samuel has exposed you to the details of several lives with Larry under various incarnations, you grasp the fact that he has been a rather stubborn person for many lifetimes. It may take extra work.

As to what you can do while he is still alive, I really don't think there is much you can do. I don't think he is going to be all that much aware of who you are, why you are there, or if you're there at all. He may have an old memory of who you are and how you fit into his life. Just don't be upset if you find him greatly incapacitated. It's not a pretty situation. In fact, it's hard for me to visit him, because he's under a lot of pain and mental confusion.

I know Larry's not going to last long. I think, Beverly, you will be back in Milwaukee later this year. So, I'm glad you've got a book project that will be portable as you drive up there. I'm sorry I can't give you a brighter forecast, but I want you to continue on with your projects, remembering that goal is very important. In a sense, Larry and I are just some additional spice to the meal that you're preparing. I guess we are all preparing for others who are willing to accept and appreciate what we are trying to communicate. I thank you for that.

I'm happy and free to go anywhere to join any cause I want. I'm thrilled my spirit guide Toby helps me, keeps me informed, and is alert. The feedback I'm getting is that everyone is pleased with the way you and I are developing. I don't want to say that I can hardly wait until you get here so I can brag about you, but that's also part of me. [*chuckles*]

Don't misinterpret; I don't want you to come anytime soon. Play out your cards the way they should be played from your point of view. Samuel is there to help you. Do not be sad when it is time to leave. Yes, you'll be sad for a moment, but good things will happen.

B: Is that one of the messages you're trying to instill in Larry?

E: Well, yes, but he's so not ready to hear that yet. It's a task I'm glad to do, but I don't love doing it. I wish I didn't have to, but it's on my plate. This is what I accepted, so that's what I do.

B: How else do you spend your time? I'm assuming you can divide yourself up, and there is enough time there for dancing.

E: Oh, I get to dance a lot—all kinds of dance. It's my good hobby. I wish you would space your time better and find a good hobby. I see your eyes are red and overworked. Work it out and do the best you can with the handicaps you have loaded on yourself. We always knew you were an obsessive person, so that hasn't changed. [*laughs*]

B: Is there anything I'm forgetting to ask you or tell you? Your pastor friend emailed me, asking if I have been in communication with you. I have not responded yet because I wanted your opinion about me "outing" you so soon. I know I will be asked again.

E: Just play it by ear. Tell her what feels helpful without making rules. Do the best you can. There are no *wrong* answers. You're finally getting that through your head. Just go with whatever feels right at the moment.

I wanted to let you know I'm pleased you'll be going to Milwaukee. It's not as nice a season for the beauty of Wisconsin, but it's good that you will be able to stay at Eastcastle and fun for me to go with you on an emotional trip down memory lane where I used to live.

B: We've got grieving to do. Neither of us can just hop from one world to the other without emotional attachment to the life we are leaving. But that's all good, too.

E: Yes, without that attachment, it would also be sad.

I'm hoping you have good speed with writing this independent transitions book of yours. I know Samuel would be happier if it were easier. Just listen to what little techniques he keeps trying to feed you because you asked for remedial work for authors. That was a smart move.

Your book will be very helpful for people who are open to this kind of thing on Earth so they have some kind of information in the various ways you have been able to communicate with us on this side. At this point I don't think you know how you've been communicating or the variety of ways available to you. Not everything is on the conscious level.

But if you could relax, it would be such a help. Figure out how to relax into it. Remember what Timingo, Kym's guide, said, if somebody comes who you don't want to talk to or listen to their nonsense, just flick him away like a gnat and get on with what *you* want. Don't fall into a panic.

I think that's all I have to say, so, Beverly, I'm sorry I didn't visit you more often, but because we were so accustomed to living our lives apart, I knew you would not be offended if I wasn't there every moment when I first crossed over. I want to thank you again for helping me adjust in the various ways you did.

B: It was wonderful talking to you, Elaine. I wish you all the best. I don't know if you'll decide to come to your memorial, but you have the option of declining. If you would like to come along with me and clue me with people's names, I'd be grateful. Keep me informed of what you would like.

Give my regards to all assembled there. Goodbye.

These are the private thoughts of Beverly the evening of May 6, 2018 in Milwaukee following the afternoon memorial service for her sister:

I spent the early part of the day in my guest room on the first floor of Bradford Terrace in Eastcastle Retirement Home continuously trying to write an outline for my part of the planned event. Previous attempts at home had not been fruitful. Likewise here! I had not felt good about talking about us as kids from mother's extensive baby book comments—too long and for what purpose?

We did lots of family parties and trips, but Elaine and I were three years apart in age. As youth we hung around kids our own ages, not each other. We had few mutual friends. After Elaine graduated from high school, she and I usually lived in different states attending schools. I couldn't find anything here to write about—any more than I found at home.

It wasn't until the death of our parents that we really bonded as middle-aged women. The older we got, the closer I felt to Elaine and was concerned for her quality of life. But my assignment for the memorial service was to talk about Elaine's early life. My mind was blank. I felt like I was letting down the pastor and Elaine.

To refresh myself, I took a break for a sentimental grand tour of Eastcastle, particularly the assisted living section and the fourth floor independent living apartment where Elaine and Larry had lived. As I walked through the building, I was surprised by how many people I remembered and interacted with as being a part of Elaine and Larry's life—but also mine! Her living here was part of my life, too.

As I looked around, I noticed how the building was starting to show a hint of wear in this fresh, smartly designed residence. I was happy my family had moved in at the beginning and enjoyed its ambiance. I was pleased I could help Elaine make their unit attractive to the eye. I was proud of our collaboration and her discerning artistic choices. Whether it was house museums, art galleries, or ballet theaters, Elaine was a wonderful companion who was nourished by the arts.

Once I leave Eastcastle this May, I will never come back. Sadly, that was the message I was getting while driving to Wisconsin and as I strolled around the retirement home. I said goodbye to the memories and even to the favorite pictures on the wall and the furnishings I had loved and I knew Elaine had enjoyed. When slowly walking through each public room, I felt its importance in our lives. This was truly the end of an era for both of the Hafemeister sisters.

I was unable to write anything to be read at the service until I thought ... well, the elephant in the room was that I had not been able to acknowledge my current task—that of moving forward, leaving the unfinished work, dropping it, and then moving into the future. I should be honest about it. The moment I switched from trying to find jolly, interesting memories, I felt honest and free. The finality of the memorial service along with summarizing my sister's contribution to this world is what I had been dreading. I still had not been able to flick that grief switch yet.

In my preparation for driving to Milwaukee from Cincinnati, I found myself thinking many times things like, "I should stay a day later so I can shop at Bayshore for new clothes for Elaine." I would catch myself thinking, "Oh that's right. She's not in that physical body anymore!" Those were indications that I had not adjusted to her current conditions, and I wasn't ready to let go of it. At a deeper level, I hadn't processed the fact that this phase of the Elaine life was over and she had moved on. On a surface level, I was fine with her having moved on and was happy she had because she was pleased she had completed her work here.

I wrongly thought I wouldn't have to deal with grief in her case because we had spoken so often since her death now that she was on the other side. I found that not to be true. I was still grasping and hanging on to our old, established relationship, thus I feared I might be holding her back. I wasn't ready to walk through that exit door yet. The only time I felt content in speech writing was to say out loud where I really was mentally. I never did end up writing anything on paper—so different than for Dad's memorial in the 1970s when I not only wrote my message (filled with my absorption of the wisdom of Rev. Herb's teaching), but rehearsed it from the church pulpit.

I counted twenty-five people attending Elaine's memorial. Eastcastle's hall was setup with tables, chairs, roses, and an abundant lunch. Guests included our 95-year-old Aunt Catherine and our cousin. Elaine's church organist played ballet music on the piano and sang two songs. Her pastor conducted a thoughtful tribute to Elaine and invited others to share their memories. I was thrilled so many people spoke about Elaine in front of the group when given the opportunity.

The pastor said Larry preferred to introduce himself and read his own sentiments, but he got stuck for a very long time. People were wonderfully patient and polite to sit quietly until he could find the words and then read his prepared script. Such a gift of patience they gave him. That's life as it is now—filled with pathos and embarrassment when you're older and seeing death coming your way.

Now Larry is living alone at Eastcastle on the skilled care floor. When his time comes, the message I am getting is that I may not choose to speak, I would either decline the offer or not be able to attend. I don't know what that prediction is, but certainly, I will never again experience Milwaukee as I have in the past. Yet, when Larry leaves, I want him to have a proper memorial.

It saddens me that if I go out tomorrow to enjoy the lake and the town, it will probably be the last of my memories of Milwaukee. I frittered away the opportunities to enjoy Milwaukee when I lived here. I had such a terribly closed attitude when I moved from Detroit in 1953. I guess it was what I agreed to experience. Yet, the other day I was heartened to be caught in a large traffic jam due to a friendly neighborhood block party along the lakeshore. It was reminiscent of my generation of the past. The same bubbly energy was shared by both the older and newer generations. Wonderful!

I sensed that Larry and Elaine's closest couple friends, Joe and Cynthia, would no longer be part of my life. It was Cynthia who said how much she appreciated my words because she was still dealing with the recent death of her elder brother. Since cold weather bothers them both, they will most likely be spending more time in the south.

Reader, at this point I invited any guide or higher self connected to Elaine or me to speak if they want. My spirit guide Samuel responded:

S: Beverly, I don't know what you are so sad about. The memorial didn't appear to be a sad celebration. I think people went away very happy and pleased that so many spoke. Everybody saw what they needed to see. Each saw according to what their veil allowed them to see in the relationship between Elaine and Larry. One lady saw their relationship as a role model for herself. Some people, like you and Cynthia, saw the pain of separation from a sibling. That's why we didn't ask you to concentrate on any particular point of view. But what you did and others did was to say their piece of the puzzle. That's exactly what we wanted you to do.

We on this side see it as a very successful and useful growth experience for all who attended. We would like you to think of it that way, too. We are glad you said similar things to Larry. We're glad you went up to his room afterwards because he was feeling sad and a bit of a failure when he messed up reading that one paragraph twice and was slow to start. But, by you talking to him and saying, "No big deal. Nobody seemed upset by that. It gave them a chance to think of their own life with Elaine."

We're glad you went up there to make him feel better. As expected he's in grief. You said a word or two to him when you first arrived about grief and how things are different. You gave him an opportunity to think of it in a different light. That's all you can do. You know all about bringing horses to water. (You can't make them drink, but you can offer them an opportunity). That's all you did; and it was perfect.

No, the event was not professionally slick and polished; but had it been, it wouldn't have been heard. It was what was needed for the people who were in attendance. So, be of good cheer as far as the success of the memorial. *We thank you.*

B: I don't know who "we" is, but you make me feel better. Thank you.

Now my special concern is, "How is Elaine with this?" If she would like to talk at this time, it would be fine.

T: No, I don't think she's ready yet. She's a bit choked up about it. She herself hadn't realized how important she was to people; and it's now just reaching her—so many of the little things she had forgotten about herself. Things other people remember and were grateful for and have become an inspiration to those who attended. How they were lucky to be in the "orbit" of that person so they could enjoy that. Everything is bittersweet and that's okay. Elaine is working her way through that grief.

B: I appreciate hearing that because she didn't want it turned into something sentimental. But, for some, maybe it was. You are right, everybody needed to hear what they heard. Is there anything more?

S: We'll talk to you when you're sleeping tonight. Yes, I think it's smart not to drive back on Monday. Tuesday should be better. Please watch what you are eating. You're getting a lot of sugar. Watch the Dairy Queen. It's your health, Beverly.

B: Thank you, guys. Hello to everybody.

Monday

Did not sit by the lake. I decided to stay near Larry at Eastcastle. Found Elaine's ashes stored in Larry's closet to be buried in my backyard with Larry's ashes when he dies. He made that request; and I was willing to grant his wish.

Tuesday

Made wonderful time driving through Chicago. Apologized to Samuel, but I stopped two times that day for a Dairy Queen blizzard—my farewell travel treat for the six decades of driving that Chicago route home to both Michigan and Ohio.

Thanks to knowing my genealogy, over the years as I drove through Chicago's south side, I always picked up a hitchhiker, my Dad, where, as a college student, he met a pretty beautician who was destined to be my mother. We'd chat telepathically until we got to the Chicago downtown "L" where he'd drop off. What fun! I'll miss those visits during my long drive home.

After arriving back in Cincinnati from the memorial service

for my sister Elaine, this was my debriefing session with Kym:

Beverly (B), Elaine (E), Kym (K), Samuel (S)

B: At the memorial service while looking at their old wedding photographs, Larry stated, "I valued Elaine for her mind. I never realized how beautiful she was."

Their friend snapped a picture of Elaine last autumn all dressed up seated in her wheelchair, but to me she looked extremely ill. I wondered if I should send Larry a picture of her at a younger age. Would the two of them standing together at their wedding help them to connect now and be appreciated? From the other side, Elaine tells me she is trying to contact him these days.

K: I'm asking Samuel if you sending a picture of Elaine to Larry would help.

S: Yeah, you can easily do that, but you're doing that for yourself. You're giving him an option to remember when she was young and beautiful. It's appropriate because it's a gift to share her youth and help trigger that memory.

Larry is practical and he remembers her as seen in the later picture. That's what he remembers her to be. He still sees her as beautiful in how he relates to her. You shouldn't focus on him remembering her only as old. He never really saw her as old and sickly. Long-term marriage partners see each other completely differently than you on the outside. That's how he knows her to be; that's his familiar. The woman in the wedding picture is no longer his familiar.

He has confessed to you on two occasions he wanted to connect with her, but found there was no "her" to answer. When a letter comes in the mail that he doesn't know how to handle, he can't ask her opinion. And that's where it's left—silence. Maybe that's the best place for it to be left.

He's such a practical guy. If he had a dream and Elaine showed up as young, he wouldn't relate to her. He has to relate to her in the way that is most familiar to him, as an older woman. That's how you related to your dad—the old familiar personality you both could identify.

B: So, I'm trying to decide: is sending a wedding picture the best thing?

S: Would it have the impact you're trying to achieve, which is to offset the old lady image he has in his head? Well, no. But it's where he is and wants to be.

B: When he connects, it will be with the fragile body she was in at the end.

S: Bev, you're not getting it. He didn't see her as you do. He sees her as *his* Elaine. You're forcing the vision of what you saw. You want to remember Elaine as young and vivacious; Larry wants familiar. He's practical; you're not. You want to remember her before all this illness.

B: Yes, because I want her to energize herself back to where she was. That suggests to me that I have not grieved sufficiently.

S: No, you're crying now. You're in your process now. There is finality in this last trip. You started your process of grieving, now let it express itself whenever it needs to. Grieve the humanness of her, not the Elaine you are currently connected to on a different level.

For Larry, it's the daily reality that she's not there to help him deal with the mail. Is she ready for dinner? First thing in the morning, is she up? She's the first and the last person he wants to talk to each day. He's *constantly* living his grief! You're just starting.

B: Because I'm a long distance person. It was not unusual for us to go several months without conversing because we never lived in the same state as adults.

S: And with her increasing sickness, Elaine could not speak, so phones were a problem—a lot of long, silent gaps. Your grieving was different than Larry's grieving. Let him do his stuff.

B: I don't want to impede him.

S: If you want to send him a picture of his wedding, do it; but it's you healing you. It will not be harmful; it's just another level of realization. Memories. Maybe that's where he's shifting into.

B: Because there were a couple of faded pictures on his window sill. I think that's what hit me so hard after she was gone how outstandingly beautiful Elaine was at that time. Elaine was so modest, I don't think she even cared or wanted to be noticed.

K: Larry never saw her beauty because that would make him wonder why such a beautiful woman would want to be with him. Like a man who marries a model; he's always afraid she will leave him for someone handsome. They set themselves up for constant anxiety. Larry didn't bring up that classic fear. Instead, he focused on her mind, her personality, and who she was. He came to the marriage with a real honesty of not falling in love with her beauty. That's why he doesn't see her that way. He's grieving the loss of her brain.

B: I wondered if that was part of the problem with him and me. In at least two past lives, he saw me as a competitor and was intensely jealous. Those feelings probably lingered into this life.

K: Also, I think he was jealous of you in this life because many men resent the ability of women to confide in other women. Men have a hard time developing that kind of sisterhood bond with their mates.

B: That's where inadequacy pops up and lingers. Thank you for helping me.

K: Elaine just popped in and said, "What about me?" Oops! I realize I didn't ask her to come.

B: [*surprised*] I'm glad she's here! [*embarrassed to neglect the main character of my trip*] What about you? I'm assuming you walked around Eastcastle with me.

E: Yes, I enjoyed it. I even pointed out some people and things for you to recall.

B: You did? I was suspicious. Like what? Pictures—I'm going to miss some of my favorite pictures in the halls and rooms. I learned so much about interior design specifically for the elderly there. Eastcastle was well done. I didn't realize how much I loved that place and how long it had been interwoven into my own life story.

K: [*Elaine shows me you two walking through Eastcastle*] All of a sudden everything you're seeing, furniture, carpet, walls, flower pots, instantaneously disappears. BAM! Only you and she are left against a plain, brown, cardboard-box-colored backdrop. Gone without a trace!

B: [*Only Elaine and I and blank space remained. I reeled in shock for several moments.*]

E: As I reminisce about Eastcastle, much of it was a lovely time with few problems. It was a nice, comfortable, safe place to go on the road I travelled—the loss of my faculties. Many people go through what I did but never had the luxury of being taken smoothly through those stages as I was.

B: True. I've been grateful for that.

E: It was fun to see people at the memorial. It was fun to be touched by their memories, thoughts and prayers. I see how limiting I was when I said I didn't want all the attention and accolades. It was tastefully done; and I appreciated it more than I thought I would. It was the energy of being in their thoughts that felt so good.

K: She's showing me Larry. She's standing in back of his wheelchair and rubbing his back and shoulders. Her loss was profound for him. He's going to be with her very soon.

E: I was there with him because he was hurting, as I was with you.

B: What else did you like about the memorial, Elaine?

E: I liked the comradery. It's been a long time in the body since I had that much comradery around. I enjoyed that a lot.

B: Former neighbors, church people, relatives ...

E: It's nice to be remembered. I didn't realize that. I've been so focused on connecting with myself again in this transition that I hadn't looked at the impact of my life on others. So it was a real treat that changed everything and was fun. It was a nice homage. I'm really glad that everyone found some closure. I'm happy for everyone to move on to their new stage of my transition. Allow space for your grief; allow Larry to have space for his grief; and everyone there on different levels. [*vigorously brushed her hands together at a completed job*]

B: [*loud laugh*] Done!

K: How funny!

E: There is so much more for us to do together. Complete this stage so we can all move on to our new stuff. Don't worry about trying to get through to Larry. He's going to be here soon enough. Don't be concerned that Larry is not getting it. Larry will get what Larry is supposed to get, and can get, at this stage of his earthly life. Don't worry about it any longer; it's not your job. Your job is to grieve that out of you, so we can accomplish more work together. There is so much happening here. I want you to be a part of it.

K: Thank you, everybody!

B: Yes. I appreciate it.

❄ ❄ ❄

Now that we have worked on getting the past in proper perspective, it's time to look around and explore what Elaine's daily life is like on the other side.

Elaine  Chapter 5

December 12, 2018

Reader, Elaine peaked my interest the other day when she said she had some ideas for my transition book. "Don't cut it off too short. My friends and I think there is so much more you hadn't touched. I'd be happy to give you ideas of what we think you're missing. Then see if our ideas fit in with the direction you want to go."

Well, I noticed in my early drafts I only concentrated on the physical attributes of Elaine's location; that was fun, but what of her mental climate?

My youthful preconceived notion was that on the other side we all think alike. But even I have proved that notion incorrect when Nancy said she loved the mental give and take of ideas in discussion groups there. Without different viewpoints, in my opinion, there can be no pro and con discussion of subjects; ergo, no growth. Well, that's a bummer!

What other proof is there about the other side being mentally stimulating? Those from a physics background like Herb are stunned by the scientific advancements being developed there. Likewise, Josh has a mind looking for answers. Marv is engrossed in what he has learned about his past lives thanks to the Akashic Record he can research. Furthermore, he doesn't hesitate to share his new ideas with others.

Elaine, my favorite bookworm, takes opportunities to attend classes and describe her recent Earth life to expand the knowledge of others in her soul cluster. Apparently, she is at a stage where she can share suggestions. So, I invited my sister's ideas.

Beverly (B), Elaine (E), and Unknown voice (U)

B: Your contributions are welcome. I need a broad spectrum of topics from which to choose. Describing the transition period between Earth and the other side is the book's narrow scope, so I shouldn't get heavily into any complex concepts. All that is likely to come up soon enough after each new arrival is acclimated to being on the other side.

E: That's true. Here's a neutral idea—our transportation system. How do we move around? How do we get from place to place? Do all people have the same ability? Or does it depend on what life stage they are in?

B: Okay, how about locomotion? What would you like to say about that?

E: This is a sampling because it's complicated. Here we all have the ability to move ourselves to where we need or want to be with just the thought, "I need or want to see ..." Just by that thought, I am transported to them without any obvious effort. Physically we appear in front of that person. They see us; we see them.

Furthermore, everybody here knows they have more than one representation of themselves. Just because you are with one person at any given time doesn't mean that you are simultaneously no place else. You have any number of identical selves and know you are connected to all your other selves. Somehow in the back of your mind you are able to sort out where the others are assembled.

If I want to go over and talk to a person, I can decide which of my images is closest to that person or not busy at the time. I know which one to send over there. I don't get the sense there is one major image while the others are the minor, lesser powerful ones. To us they seem alike in power, authority, and direction. Seeing your image in one place is the same as seeing it in another place at the same time. They may be dressed differently to suit the occasion, but they are fully in control of what's going on. You think they are autonomous, but they are just identical.

We don't worry about where our other selves spend the time. They just sort of disappear out of sight. They don't live with us. It's sort of like a balloon that can deflate when not needed. Next morning they puff up for active duty if needed.

You need to keep in mind that in addition to yourself and your images of yourself ready to represent you, you will be exposed to your past lives who are on this side. So, you might wonder about crowding. You might think the cities are jammed, but we don't have a sense of being crowded although there are many more of us. Somehow that is all worked out so we feel comfortable in whatever setting we are in. I don't know the scientific abilities behind that phenomenon, but crowd control is not a problem.

Nobody seems to worry about locomotion as a thing you've got to have. You already have the capacity to be places. We don't bother with cars, unless you're a real hobbyist.

B: I assume there is no need for elevators. How about telephones? You're not needing telephones, telegraphs, emails, computers? Right?

E: We're so advanced that telepathic communication is incorporated into everything we do. It almost feels like a natural ability we have to communicate. Originally these modes of communication were new inventions here first before on Earth.

B: Are you suggesting things are invented on your side of the veil and eventually trickle down to Earth for use?

E: Yes, I would say ideas start here. Unfortunately, sometimes people on Earth find unkind ways to use our inventions to hurt people. Here inventions are strictly beneficial with no unkind repercussions. Of course, the misuse saddens us, because we are stuck with how are we going to get rid of the hurtful uses? How are we gonna change that? It becomes an important aspect of the work that needs to be done on this side.

B: I can appreciate why sharing ideas with us is risky business for you if you always have to play catch up because our fertile minds are bent on havoc. As you talked about the other side, I kept thinking about gravity. You have no gravity, but I wonder how do things stay on a table? Why do things stay put?

E: That's true. Somebody's got it all figured out. Things work out here just like they do on Earth except we do not have gravity or time. As somebody pointed out, to be practical we have to deal with your time because we have to schedule ourselves around what's happening on Earth. Thus, in a sense, we *are* living in time, though technically we are not.

B: Another question people are going to want to know about is: what about my deceased pets? Am I going to see them on the other side?

E: The answer is yes and no, but I'm not sure I'm qualified to answer. Sometimes the pets will want to see their humans, so they will swing through this planet we are living on just to see them temporarily. It is not a living situation where people are accustomed to living with their pets as a family member. It's up to the pets themselves to see their previous master.

Highly-evolved animals have that ability. It is usually not a factory-farm, herd animal that has never had any association with humans. They don't care to see humans. For what purpose? They would not ask since no earthly friendships had blossomed.

Yes, we have pets but they are choosing how much time they want to spend here with their human friends.

B: You're saying "home" is not their natural habitat now.

E: That's correct. [*chuckles*] I'll say it's a vacation trip for them to come here if they desire.

B: That's stunning information. Kym has said she has felt her dog romp through her life on occasion, so that's in keeping with how you describe the free will of her late dog. When Kym's cats visit, she can tell which cat it is by their walk. One cat always walked delicately placing her paws precisely with great care. The other cat walked in a wide swath like a tomboy, expecting others to get out of his way. When they come to visit Kym on Earth and jump on her lap then walk across her shoulders, there is no mystery about who they are. So, Elaine, it sounds accurate to me. In other words, the animal has the upper hand of what human they want to visit. So if your rabbit or horse visits you that means there was an affectionate bond between you.

E: Yes.

B: Is there an opinion as to whether that is good or bad? Or is that just "is"?

E: I don't know. I've not particularly heard people talk about the pros and cons. Since you, more than me, were attached to animals, and in my lifestyle now, I don't know what that could mean to you with your beloved horse Rudy. That may be totally different and an unknown that I can't answer for you.

B: I'm curious, are you living in a version of the U.S.A.? What's the community feeling like? Small townish? Or metropolitan?

E: I'm very comfortable here, which for me means small, like my beloved Shorewood!—various sized houses, pleasant green areas, charming walkable streets, tree lined roads, a placid Lake Michigan, and friendly people. It's the kind of situation I enjoyed in Shorewood. I feel at home in that environment.

For others who enjoy city life, they are the ones who go to the more populated areas. You can pick an area that gives you pleasure, I would say. You're free, just as you are in the States, to move if your interests change. If you feel like you want to be someplace else, you're free to do that. This environment is very liberating about space.

B: Is your society homogeneous or diverse with various religions, cultural beliefs, and governments?

E: From what I can see we are a mix of races, religions, social customs, and how different societies organize themselves.

B: So, in your living experience you get to meet people from different points of view. Right?

E: Yes, definitely, that is part of our training here, though we don't necessarily think of it that way. One of the basic things we do absorb as we live here is how we can get along with each other by each expressing our own points of view. To me, that is an important thing that the Earth community has not grasped. It grieves us greatly. We spend our time thinking of how we can remedy that problem for earthlings.

I mentioned how some inventions here are turned into destructive means to hurt people on Earth. That's what we think about even on the social end of things. How can we teach people to appreciate each other and have it transfer itself to Earth's societies so it becomes a benefit not a harm that twists us into warring camps of thought? Rigidity is not our intention.

B: Good luck with that one! In terms of family matters, are you able to see Mother and Dad as much as you want? I don't know how things work there. Are there Thanksgiving family dinners? Or do you have a different, larger sense of family particularly since you're aware you are living many lives together at the same time? Defining a family unit must be complex. How does that work out in daily life?

E: Yes, it is true; we have a *totally* different concept of family. For example, which Mother are you talking about? Each of my lives has a different one. My mothers are all unique; and it was important that they all *were* different because it was important for their soul growth, important for mine, and that's what's so overwhelming about readjusting to life over here. It's so much bigger than we can possibly dream and can be a big stumble for Earth folks.

As you can imagine, it totally affects how we live. On Earth we usually have one little unit of people we call family. People usually come here expecting to be possessive of the individual families they knew on Earth only to discover, "Hey, this is quite different from what I anticipated!" The family unit here is dramatically varied and larger.

Actually, it's amazing how interconnected we are. If only Earth people had a better inkling, just an inkling, of how big our family really is in terms of us living multiple lives at the same moment, it would make such a difference in the world without even introducing the idea of past lives we have already left. Basically we are related to everybody, so we've got to learn to live better together. Some may realize they still have lingering prejudices they can work on to reduce their impact later.

B: Listening to the daily news now, I see how divisive we are. It's sad.

E: But it would be nice to try to help ease the struggles of divisiveness.

B: That gives me pause. I'll use the word "worry" about what I say in this book. I'm on the same page as you.

E: Absolutely!—as you should. You are going to be greatly scrutinized so that the people with the best intentions cannot inadvertently be misquoted and misunderstood. Frankly, there are people here who are not keen on having you proceed at all, just out of fear. Their concern is somebody is going to make it worse. As you see in today's news, the problem of one person using drone technology over an airport during Christmas rush can cause a colossal, three-day shut down and disrupt society. One person's impact!

B: We're both concerned. In fact, your comments caused me to wonder about how your society chooses to govern itself. Are your officials elected? Or, are these folks appointed from a higher realm?

E: The way of making group decisions is achieved by each person having a touch-button pad to record instantaneously either a yes or no answer from the assembled folks during the meeting. If both sides of a question have merit, pick one or don't vote.

B: That method will bring you speedy results but not wise solutions without addressing the valid points each side represents. I'm shocked. Have you not been watching what's happening to us? We are destroying ourselves because we accept too many simple, half-baked answers for important, complex problems. Voting that way totally silences the gifts any deep thinkers bring to the table. You need them; they will identify the ramifications of proposed actions before you jump in with both feet.

I'm afraid we are so in love with our electronics that we are emotionally headed that way, inadvertently "dumbing down" ourselves.

E: I'm thinking of the committee that I'm told consists of wise souls tasked with helping elderly people on Earth have an easier transition by preparing them for the next phase of life. Instead of being on the forefront, this knowledge is not happening for them. The committee is following and falling behind. Older people on Earth are having a harder and harder time living a self-sustaining life taking care of their basic needs.

B: As to the book, I will do the best I can to follow the spirits with higher wisdom into the near future. Yes, it would be good to have a nice light-weight book about transitions so people know what physical conditions they are going to confront. It distresses me that equality for people is not happening on Earth, but I feel inadequate to plunge into any kind of political points of view. I confess it makes me nervous.

U: We are going to stop right here. You have just said you do not want to do this unless it is a light-weight book.

B: Who am I talking to?

U: Your superiors.

B: Is Elaine all right?

U: She's mad.

B: That's okay by me to let her express her opinion.

U: Beverly, what do you want to accomplish?

B: What I want to accomplish as I look around at people on Earth is to see people not terrified by death. We are terrified of what's going to happen to us. We're terrified we will be lost in outer space without love. Many of us know how inadequately we lead our lives, so we fear judgment.

The religion that most of us have grown up with or been exposed to has not given us accurate information nor secure feelings about what comes next. The majority of people I hear naively believe the next stage is a peaceful heaven where they don't have to do anything. Everything is provided. However, this is not true; this belief is not honestly preparing them.

U: My concern is that might encourage people to die before their time; and I heard you express that same concern.

B: Yes, that's true. My concern is some troubled people might think death is a solution. It's an unfortunate idea, because, as you mentioned, people discover they have work to do over there when they cross over. Death is not an escape. I hope that would give people pause to have second thoughts about how they address struggles in life.

We need to have people on Earth who are better informed with the reality of the next stage. Yes, life is going to be better because the more negative things are dampened down and not expressed. Yes, folks will usually be living in better circumstances, but they are oblivious to the fact that they have serious work to do on both sides—before and after physical death.

Yet, I am feeling inhibited here with old age health issues. I get worn out quickly, so it's hard for me to jump up and volunteer. I preserve my energy for things I think count. So, does that give you understanding of where my thoughts are?

U: Yes, it does. We will take it aside and think about it. We don't want to comment now, but it is something we have not dealt with sufficiently. We question whether you are the right author for this job.

B: I am willing to do the work. The book is a worthwhile cause, even if it appeals only to small groups of people. Yet, it might help set a tone for the next generation who many times will have proactive people.

U: Okay, we will take that under advisement.

B: It sounds like you are dismissing me. May I say goodbye to Elaine if that's acceptable with everyone? Or are you preferring us not to talk?

U: I don't care, but I don't know if she wants to talk. She might want to do it later when she calms down. She is impatient with us.

B: While I wait, I'm curious. Do you talk to me when I'm sleeping?

U: Yes, I have. That's why I thought I'd keep track of you today. I'm happy you had a surprise communication with your dad's former secretary, Ginny, who shouted and waved to you from a hilltop. It gladdens my heart to know you respect and appreciate this lovely lady.

B: Yes, Ginny was Dad's friendly, high-energy co-worker who took me under her wing when I was lonely after moving to Milwaukee.

U: Okay. Here's Elaine.

B: I hope I haven't made life more difficult for you, Elaine.

E: I'll get over it. In the meantime, it would be wise for us to let the higher ups debate among themselves. They know each other and know what their concerns are. We should just wait and see what happens.

We listened in on your video conference a few weeks ago to your book discussion group. Like you, I was disappointed that Bill was absent and a technology puzzle forced Salle to give up in frustration because she couldn't transmit her opinions. Now we see that technology is an ongoing problem of late.

Nothing particularly outstanding about what was said. It was a good enough start for our observations, but we had higher expectations. You sound so mid-western America, and, as expected, it reflects your views of life. That's the way it appears to us on this side. However, it might be suspicious if you talked in some other way, but for us it's the honest picture of what you believe you are living through.

Your last comment to Salle, "We're only swapping illusions after earthly death" was an important point. Even many of us here hadn't thought they might still be in an illusion—fresh and new, but still an illusion. If there was anything Earth shattering at this gathering, it was your comment.

B: I have no idea where that came from! I always think they come from me, but I don't know where they really originated.

E: Furthermore, it was okay to point out that wherever Doris went to have her spiritual experience, her event might have been totally out of the experience of anybody who heard her that class day from our location. But it is a big universe. There is no way for us to know what she experienced—not that we doubt what she experienced. It was not within our repertoire. I wanted to make that clear.

U: I don't think anyone on our committee went away particularly dejected or discouraged other than the fact only four people were there. We were hoping to get more of a variety of opinions and viewpoints.

The committee continued to attend your weekly class in hopes attendance and technology had improved. The people on this side found it interesting to see what people at an advanced age on your side are thinking about. This will help us to know what is important with this group of elders.

Upon a few return visits, the committee seems "blown away" with the quality and depth of wisdom the six elderly participants show for each other. Hence, our committee is forced to rethink your group's trajectory of information and supportive love expressed for each other. The committee is now aware that they have underestimated the capacity of some folks who are looking for more realistic spiritual nourishment in their advancing years. You have shown us respectful consideration is useful for many in their desire for continued growth.

E: Further good evidence was found when Dad and I attended your class while we, plus you Beverly in real time, were being tested to determine if we could spot the origins of our misinterpretations of attitudes. We were able to walk through it with your group's earthly assistance. Salle was the first clever one who figured out that our problem was projecting criticism back at ourselves.

Dad says to be sure to thank your class for helping us. I'm hoping some of our people here were able to witness for themselves exactly how intelligent, spiritually-minded people could receive information if we allowed them more access to what is going on over here. Here's a perfect sample of how both sides can help each other find answers.

Beverly, I'm feeling better about the committee than I did the other day. I was a little bit put out because of some changes and second thoughts from committee people who were deciders on our first day together. Anytime you get people together that's likely to happen. I underestimated the fact that, after people were alone with their thoughts, they sometimes feel a need to rethink things. That's life everywhere, I guess.

B: Yep, I've done my share of rehashing.

E: Don't fret if you backslide. Deal with things when they come up and don't let them become a festering point to be stored in your body, Bev. Now you're having to work so furiously in order to get rid of as much baggage as you can while you are in the body at the time you accumulated it. It's true. The more you can get rid of while you are at the spot where you collected it, the better and easier it is for you in the long run. So I urge you to continue doing your best to rid yourself of these old touchy points.

I see how quickly you get worn out. Be sure you're not just reminiscing and not wanting to move forward with too much acceptance with the way things are. I was able to do a lot at the end of my life that makes my life so much easier now. I don't want you to ease up on your self-discipline. If you don't take care of it now, you get stuck with it the next time around or whenever.

B: One of the hidden disadvantages of living a long life is the tendency to want or need to ease up physically. Thank you for reminding me of the down side of resting on my laurels. Gotta keep balanced in life.

E: Well, I've had my fill of "lollygagging" around on this side. It's time for me to find some meaningful work or adventure that I'd love to do. So I'm starting to look at some of these job opportunities that are available to see if there is anything that tweaks my imagination. I'm happy there are all kinds of projects going on. I look forward to doing what I can do with my skillset and interest level. I'm hunting for what appeals to me.

I feel no hesitation or need for therapy to get over any of my disease symptoms that I may have brought with me. Fortunately, all that got left behind with the body. I feel able-bodied and happy to pitch into whatever I want. I'm most grateful for that.

B: Sounds like a new beginning, a new chapter to start.

E: Yes, I had some inspiring talks today with various people. With so many options, I'm gonna have a hard time deciding what I want to do. Very happy to say I have a plethora from which to choose.

B: I'll be pleased to hear about your job-hunting experiences. I assume you and Toby talk over the direction into which you want to head. I trust you can keep job flexibility and fine tune a specialty later. In the meantime, you have so many perceptive skills that will be used wherever you find work you enjoy. I'm sure the other people will be thrilled to have you on their staff.

E: Thank you. I will use you for a reference. [*chuckles*]

B: I don't know if that's good or not! I'm told I do some outrageous things when I'm asleep and go there, particularly for costume parties. I almost wish I didn't know that since I worry about whether I am politically correct when asleep attending classes, meetings, and parties.

E: Many relatives speak fondly of you and always express interest in how you're doing.

B: It's nice to be remembered. I think I'll say goodnight until later when we both have learned a little bit more.

E: Yes, I will say goodbye, too. I don't know if that's good or bad for us not to be bothered with sleeping! [*laughter*] We just talk directly and don't have to develop dream symbolism that might get misinterpreted. In the long run, we're getting our dreams directly without the confusion or challenge of figuring messages out like many Earth people must.

B: For me, not sleeping eliminates the possibility of dreams, which probably is not good. Dreams take work both for the creative storyteller and the receiver, but the other side keeps pumping them out, so it must be working sufficiently well to keep it as a form of communication. Whatever works. See ya, Sis.

In the next section of the book we travel back in time to join Elaine's husband, Larry. As he notices his wife's decline, he retains his feisty attitude toward life. You'll see how this outspoken procrastinator proves to be a headstrong challenge for even his spirit guides.

Part 5 Larry

1952 University of Michigan Grad
Mechanical Engineer
Author's Brother-in-law

Larry and Elaine together from 1966 - 2018

Larry  Chapter 1

July 15, 2017

I begin this section of the book by going back in time to when both Elaine and Larry were still alive. One July Saturday afternoon while Kym was away shopping, I was at the kitchen counter feeling an increasingly heavy weight press down on my head. To deal with my discomfort, I sat down in the living room with my tape recorder.

Al (A), Beverly (B), Unknown voice (U)

B: I think someone's trying to get my attention. I do not like the feeling, so if you've got something to say, speak up. Let's get on with it!

U: Why are you suddenly all in a hurry when I've been trying to get your attention for a long time; and you have been ignoring me?

B: I didn't know anyone was there.

U: I'm somebody you need to talk to because I'm somebody who can help you, but you haven't reached out to me at all.

B: Are you offended?

U: Yes, a little, but it's not your fault. You're just another ignorant person.

B: [*inclined to reject conversations with disrespectful spirits*] Well, I don't think you need to talk to me with that attitude.

U: I have to. I've been sent here by someone that I owe a favor to and you're it. So hang on for this ride. I'm not going to repeat myself.

B: Well, obviously you don't want to do this.

U: Right. I've got a rotten attitude, but you need to know what I have to say. All your problems are related to me.

B: Sounds like you have some kind of a confession to make.

U: Yes, I do; and it's not easy for me because I feel guilty. They're telling me, you're doing a lot of diligent work to get some knowledge out to the masses. I'm getting the blame for slowing your work down and bringing an end to your life sooner than they want you to go.

B: So this is your bothersome guilt. Say what you want to say. I think it's unburdening time for both of us.

May I ask who you are and your part in this life?

U: I am your brother-in-law. You know my name as Larry.

B: [*hitting a sore spot*] This is not happy news for either one of us. [*crying*] I'm sorry there has been so much pain between us. I didn't want it to happen.

A: [*Larry's guide, Al, approaches*] Beverly, you're not getting a true picture here. I'm not forcing Larry to do anything. I'm *suggesting* he recognize this opportunity to release some old karma. But his stubborn personality, like an obstinate child, feels, "You're making me do this!" Consequently, he shows up with this crabby attitude toward you. He's not being forced to do anything—far from it.

Not intended as judgment against Larry, it's to help you understand the basic personality of Larry's soul—strong, determined, self-focused. Please understand there is great happiness and fulfillment in Larry's soul except when he's asked to do something he doesn't want to do.

In some lives his soul's personality is diluted; in other lives it's full strength. Each person chooses the dilution to accomplish that lifetime's goal. It's his M.O. just like you, Beverly. Your soul is the strong warrior risk-taker personality. Larry's version is not diluted; Beverly's version is.

B: I think back to his early marital days and remember the demonstrative, loving, cheerful Larry. Elaine responded well to that happy person.

A: Wrong issue! His resistance is himself when asked to work on his flaws. For eons he has avoided working on himself; and it weighs him down. He struggles to deal with the raw, real issue of his love for you and ...

B: [*As I typed these words I was overwhelmed with tears of sadness and puzzlement.*] Years ago when I finally realized I loved Larry, I wanted to know our backstory. So far I can only see past lives where we harmed each other and ourselves.

A: You're both in the end phase of these lives and want to get rid of baggage. More powerful and better is to resolve injury in this Earth life rather than wait until you are both on the other side.

B: Al, I thought when we are on the other side we didn't have the lower emotions. Is Larry's soul on the other side? Why is he demonstrating such negative behaviors?

A: Larry's soul is currently in an incarnation, so he can connect to all that emotional negative behavior. Larry's soul showing obstinate behavior is not on the other side; he is connected here to an Earth life. Therefore, his soul can easily tap into those lower energies.

Here's an exercise I think might help you. Go back to the time and emotion of when you identified the problem with Larry. Think about how he might view events you shared. By coming to compassion for Larry be sure to sort out the stuff that doesn't belong in that category with him.

Do like you did with the Marv exercise. Have conversations with yourself. It's *not* what you can consciously do *with* Larry.

Instead, this is *your* internal work about this issue. Work through your veiled *emotions* of past events with Larry, then tackle your veiled *thoughts*. When done, ask, "Where am I storing my resentment in my body around Larry and that situation?" Release it, and you will release illness and pain. You'll need to do that many times. The extra benefit is it will help Larry's soul also.

❋ ❋ ❋

Days later Kym was inspired to channel these thoughts for me:

Beverly (B), Kym (K)

K: Beverly, you have a tendency to view your sister as a victim. Consider Elaine's goal as a feminine woman was to understand a left brain, logical engineer man. She took her role of mate seriously and did not want to criticize. Her perception might be: I picked a strong male because I am knowledgeable about how men think. I know how my husband thinks, whereas my sister is artistically logical but not as an engineer. I understand my sister because we are women. Males and females have two different ways of viewing life, which adds to the conflict they share.

B: Furthermore, any non-traditional, religious concept baffles Larry.

K: You are into spirituality, including things like homeopathy. Because of his traditional views, talking with Larry is uncomfortable. Therefore, coming from your perspective, you *judge* him. You have concluded you have nothing in common. When you come up with alternative therapies for Elaine, he can't go down that road. You took offense to his objections. He wasn't necessarily rejecting you; he was rejecting your philosophy.

B: Because I wasn't scientific enough. At one time Larry, according to Samuel, despised me. Was that hyperbole?

K: You pushed his "I don't understand her" button. If he doesn't understand, he rejects.

B: I wanted to respond, "Of course, you don't understand; you're a rigidly thinking engineer."

K: You roll up all your irritation with him into one ball, thus deem *everything* he does as wrong.

B: Yes, he becomes my dumpster of things I don't endorse. I don't bother anymore to sort it out.

K: What does that do? It makes baggage!

Instead, every day you've got to say, "Where else in my body am I holding resentment about Larry that's ready to be released?" See what pops up when you ask. Everyone's got resentments packed away. Start releasing the simpler ones coming to the surface while you are on the Earth.

Bev, a guy just entered the room to say the hex he put on you is now coming due. He needs to help you and himself. I think this might be Larry, but he doesn't want to talk through me. He wants to talk directly to you.

❋ ❋ ❋

The next morning Beverly channeled this conversation:

Beverly (B), Larry (L), Spirit Guides (SG)

L: This is your brother-in-law, Larry, who is asking to communicate with you on the *unconscious* level because in my current mental and physical state it's the only way we have to communicate and improve our relationship. So, we will go with what we have if that's okay.

B: Yes, that's fine.

L: I hear your prayers for me, your prayers for Elaine, and your prayers for yourself. I know that you have heard some of the history of our relationship in past lives when I was extremely jealous of your successes. While in your sorceress life, my ordering the poisoning of your toddler son doesn't make me happy, at least I know it is helping you to know where I'm coming from in this current life. I appreciate that information is out of the bag, so I don't have to deal with that particular part of self-confession. I'm glad that period is over. I don't know where that will take me or us, but I see that talking openly is an advantage already.

B: Because you have come to me, I'm going to assume there is something particular on your mind. If so, would you like to express it now?

L: I wouldn't like to, but they're still pressuring me that this is a good opportunity to get rid of some of my baggage that I keep bringing to each lifetime. As you said, I am a logical person and see that as a reasonable course of action. And you are absolutely right; I do see it as an opportunity I should not pass on at this time.

I truthfully feel miserable and dishonest with myself. I'm lonely. I can't hear what Elaine is saying because she talks so softly. I get mad and yell at her because of her infirmity. There is nothing I can do with it or about it.

B: Well, let's think about the problem. What are Elaine's abilities now? Send your thoughts to her in your head like you are to me. At least you'd be communicating, not on the surface, but you'd have a grounding and commonality between the two of you that might be felt. If you can communicate with me, than you can do the same with Elaine because she's able to talk in her head. She's had so much experience in this life because she wasn't a person who wanted to force her way into a conversation.

Try it, Larry. Start talking to her in your thoughts between the two of you, or try other modes of communication. I think you'll find she loves you very much and stays faithfully loyal. She's a gem.

The second topic is your need for a hearing aid. Years ago you decided never to get one, so it was almost guaranteed you'd eventually feel lonely. When people can't hear, they begin to feel they are no longer in on what's happening; they commonly feel left out. Sort out current options and decide what's best for you. What is needed—a hearing aid for you or voice amplification for Elaine? It's your choice.

Larry, please think of me as a friend. Leaving your independent apartment was a hard transition for you. I understood your meaning when I looked around and saw from your point of view that there weren't many people for you to talk to on your new floor.

[*feeling insecure yet pushing on, Beverly extends her reach*] I don't know where we are at this stage. Is there a spirit guide like Samuel or Al around?

SG: Yes. We see you have attempted to communicate and help him. We also knew you were uninformed about this type of connection but later became aware you are uninformed. However, it's time to begin your day, so we will let you go and discuss this further independently and perhaps together.

We want you to know that we've taken your suggestion of a week ago, Beverly. After your night work, you and we have gone to where Larry is and have made an effort to talk to him. I think you'll agree this is a difficult case and may not be successful because he's so stubborn and ill prepared to help himself. We can't figure it out and know you can't either. Why would a guy deliberately hurt himself?

B: Since I have no memory of my night work, I'm unaware of what transpired between us. Does Larry know he's hurting himself?

SG: We're not sure. We were hoping you would make that point stronger to him, which you kinda did. We've got to be blunt with him.

❋ ❋ ❋

A few days later, I started getting pressure on my head and grabbed my recorder:

Beverly (B), Larry (L)

B: Would you like to go ahead and talk please?

L: Yes, I will. This time it's Larry with my friend Beverly …

B: [*silently stunned, so I only thought, "What am I hearing? … my friend, Beverly!"*]

L: ... who I have been visiting all this time—which means yesterday. I've been traveling with you to see what you've been up to and how you spend your time. I found it interesting.

I appreciate you, Beverly, taking me to your session with Susan Gibson who did the energy work on both of us. I appreciate that experience and found it pleasant. I thank you and I should have thanked Susan for the treatment. Please tell her I appreciated it. Maybe I was being too protective by asking you *not* to share my comments with Susan. I knew my whispered words of thanks crossed your mind as you were leaving her. I should have said go ahead and tell her that I was appreciative, but I hesitated.

You have things to do now, but I wanted you to know that I have released my hex on you and wish you all the best and success in carrying out the endeavors you are doing. Please, know that I have no ill feelings towards you, and I hope you have none towards me.

B: Thank you for that. No, I hold no bad thoughts of you, but emotional feelings are harder to control.

As you have probably witnessed, I've been working on my problem of releasing past events. I know from personal experience what a tough road this work is—to see what transpired in those past lives and to find remedies that release them. It *is* work.

I appreciate you letting me know you have removed that hostility, and I'm grateful for both of us. We can now go ahead as friends and see what we can do to help each other wherever we are, whichever side of the veil. Before you go, is there something I can do for you to make it easier for you as we go forward in time?

L: I will let you know as things occur to me. Remember the conscious Larry does not know about this. There will be a lot of backsliding because I see now how difficult I am in my really grouchy mood. I've certainly been there a long time, so please forgive me when I have eruptions. From my point of view, I will do my best to keep myself updated on your activities. Thank you for asking. Feel free to call upon me anytime.

B: Should I go through Samuel? Is that how the procedure works?

L: No, call me directly. I knew a few days ago that you were able to talk with Elaine by just putting her in mind. That will work for us, too.

B: Very good! Pleased to hear that. Thank you for all your hard work, Larry. Goodbye now.

❊ ❊ ❊

September 11, 2017

Two months later I heard an urgent voice, "Please turn up the volume so I can be heard better. I want you to get this information, but I don't have a lot of time to spend with you. This is Larry himself. Elaine's asleep in her room across the hall, but I need to talk to someone so I want you to know I'm not doing very well, but I'm glad to know you are thinking of me. I can't seem to concentrate and regret being so slow at getting my earthly responsibilities organized. I feel myself slipping away. Frankly, I'm afraid.

Would you please tell me what you know about the other side? I feel like I will be leaving this Earth plane and moving on to the next phase of life. I have no idea what to expect. I suspect you know more than I do or at least you seem to be more in tune with what's more realistic than what we've been taught in the churches. Beverly, please tell me what to expect."

Beverly (B), Larry (L), Samuel (S)

B: [*feeling incompetent*] Oh, gee, Larry, I'll do my best to help you. Here's a quick summary of what I've been told. We are spiritual energy surrounded by others who love us greatly. When our physical body gives out, we go back to our energy body and our life goes on.

Your spirit guide Al remains your best buddy on both sides

of the veil and will assist you to make good decisions as you think through choices. Whatever is decided, you can organize yourself into a path that is useful and helpful to you, your neighbors, and friends. Once you've readjusted to the freedom of your spiritual body, it's time to get active again.

You can meet your spirit guide in this life while still in the physical body. If you would like to meet that person now, Larry, what you might do is, (I'm assuming you're in a sleep state now) just look around and see if there is a familiar face or familiar energy who would like to step forward and introduce himself to you. I'm told people always seem to recognize this person because that person has been with them in many lifetimes. So that may be the case in your situation, too.

Does that help?

L: Yes, that's exactly what I needed to know because there is such a person here with me now. I think you were introducing me to that person. When I go, I want you to tell Elaine that I have met that person and am being assisted and escorted and feel very calm now.

B: Good. You and he will continue to work together. You might recognize him as the guide who helped you plan your Larry life. In some cases people make earlier plans, so, at death, they go immediately to another phase, *the ghost level*, because they've decided they want concentrated learning—like an advanced crash course. Yet even there, ghosts have access to helpful people and spirit guides ready to advise them if they ask.

Most times the recently deceased proceed past the ghost level without even being aware of its presence and are greeted with joy on the other side by family. Loved ones and friends they knew in their lifetime celebrate these reunions. After the parties, there is a period of transitional adjustment to life on the other side.

Once that period is over, people want to get together to discuss their relationship with each other and learn from their experiences at an emotional distance. We go on to help each other through the multiple next phases of life and have a lot of input into what happens next. Hope that helps.

At 9:00 p.m. that evening I might have been thinking, "I wonder how it's going with Larry." My spirit guide, Samuel, retorted, "Beverly, everything is in flux—just like you and me."

Oops! I have been weighing, vacillating, and struggling with this same death issue myself for a year and a half after hearing my own cardiologist predict I would live only two more years. I don't know how many of these conversations with Samuel have been on the conscious or unconscious level. I knew I was unwittingly playing a serious game in my head of checking off items on two lists—either pro or con physical life. I couldn't turn my opinions off!

S: Larry has been talking to his spirit guide about the immediate future—whether to live or die now or later. They are discussing the options freely thanks to you introducing Larry to his guide, whom he recognized from past lives. That freed him up to take seriously the value of this discussion—whether there is more to be learned at this stage on the Earth side or on the other side.

Larry came to you because his soul came to him and suggested he speak to you. That was possible because you and his soul have befriended each other over the last few weeks. Without that connection, this meeting with Larry's spirit guide would not have happened—especially in the rush of this eleventh hour of his life.

Beverly (B), Larry (L), Samuel (S),

A month later, October 16, 2017:

L: This is Larry. I want you to know I've made the decision to leave at this time. I've talked it over with my soul; and we feel it's the best move. So, I'm letting you know that this will happen in the near future and for you to be prepared to go to Wisconsin to be with Elaine so she can get over her grief as easily as possible. We've taken a lot of time to think this through; and we've come to the conclusion that it's better for all concerned if I go first and that I go now. Elaine is in agreement with this decision, so she knows on the subconscious level I will be leaving her. She will have a short time to be alone.

I'm sorry to do this. It's not going to be an easy time for any of you because there are many things that have not been finalized in closing up my part of the estate. This is a forewarning that there is going to be a lot of confusion and dissension between all the people involved. I'm sorry to do this, but I guess that's all a part of the decision to leave at this time. I do this regretfully because I realize I'm going to cause a lot of problems for a great many people. I'm afraid it's going to cost you a lot both financially and emotionally. I hope you will be able to think kindly of me when I'm gone.

B: I don't know what else to say. I feel like I'm in unchartered territory. Unless you or someone else has something to add … Would someone like Samuel like to add a p.s. to this or just leave it for now?

S: Whatever you want, Beverly. I can offer you condolences now, but there's going to be so much to be done in Milwaukee; and I'm afraid it's going to mean winter months up there. I hate to say months, but that's exactly what it's going to be because of the uncertainty of the legal papers.

❋ ❋ ❋

A fortnight later, October 28, 2017

Samuel (S), Beverly (B)

S: You are more important to us staying in Ohio and your team here would prefer you not to go to Wisconsin at all. However, missing any memorial service is not likely to happen due to your respect for both of your family members.

B: During Larry's mid to late 80s, he had some stays in the hospital to enhance his health. All such events happened while Elaine was alive. One serious heart valve operation I believe changed the order in which Elaine and Larry died. While I was sleeping one night, I was invited to attend a family conference. The next morning I awoke deeply grieving from an unknown sadness. Without memory of the meeting, I entered the first stages of grief over my sister's decision to die first, before Larry. Yet, I knew it was the better order of events for both of them. As you read, January 10 became the evening of Elaine's departure.

July 19, 2018

Beverly's Journal:

Months later, with Elaine gone, Larry was living a lonely existence. So let me digress from Larry's health to mine during this time frame. I'd been warned by Samuel, Marv, Elaine, and soulmate Herb to spend less time on spiritual work and more time grounded on Earth. Energy worker Susan also has been complaining to me that I'm not grounded enough.

Increasingly I've been dizzy and almost felt I could float off the Earth. Kym reminded me that a good way to get grounded was to go barefoot on grass. So today I sat in the driveway with my feet on the grass and began to grieve for that complex person in my life—Larry.

Sitting at the driveway edge, I got a chill on both lower legs with the message from his friends that I was to play a part in Larry's transition, so staying grounded was important. If I escort Larry part of the way to the other side, I must turn back when told. I emphatically said "Yes! I want to write about his journey, too." I knew my roles in this event were both as observer and participant.

I was told when the time came to escort Larry, I was to wear boy's PJs because (previously unknown to me) I am Larry's favorite brother from another life; and that's who he would see. As we travel away from Earth, I would morph back into Beverly to demonstrate to Larry about multiple lives. (See, Reader, I told you: *those spirit guides never miss an opportunity to teach us.*) Then I was to return back to Earth as he proceeds on. Okay, that sounded interesting for the book. Let's go for it!

I heard nothing further from the other side, but a series of emails from his pastor (a friend and medical power of attorney for Larry all rolled into one) included the following updates and a phone call:

> 7/19/18, Thursday 12:08 pm. Just want you to know. I saw Larry Tuesday the 17th and he was doing very well, however, today he is unresponsive and dying.
>
> 7/20/18, Friday 9:26 am. I'm surprised at the suddenness of this turn of health. Most unexpected! Will keep you updated.
>
> 7/20/18, Friday 4:31 pm. I saw him this afternoon. He's a little worse today and he has lots of gunk in his chest but he's comfortable.

7/21/18, Saturday 4:15 pm. Journal entry:

The pastor phoned me to say Larry just died in his room at Eastcastle. He had hospice care with drugs only during the last three days when his breathing became extremely labored, but he had not been sent to the hospital. She remarked how fast he went downhill and could hear a rattle in his throat when breathing. He died quickly and believed he had no motive to live without Elaine.

So the end of my family's Earth journey has come. I felt empty. Appallingly I was immediately thrust into dispensing with the material remains in Larry's room though I was in Ohio. The retirement home procedure wanted his room empty within twenty-four hours. Where do you want things to go?

Larry's body was sent to the crematorium. The precision, pen, line drawings were to go to their pastor friend. The handmade miniature dresser that Larry's grandfather made to win the hand of his sweetheart was to go to Larry's friend (and eventually to a long lost cousin). Elaine's Great Aunt Louise's gold-leaf mirror, Elaine's wedding ring, and photographs were to be sent to me. The bank is in charge. Eastcastle wants you out PDQ!

I had recognized for over a decade that Eastcastle was the home of *my* heart, too, so I grieved once more the loss to me of this lovely place. Poof! It wasn't real—just as Elaine showed me after she and I walked through most of the place before *her* memorial service in May. Poof—total blank brown, not a trace of a keepsake memory! Nothing gentle or gradual about it! BAM.

❄ ❄ ❄

July 22, 2018, Sunday mid-day, I felt the bottom of my leg tingle and asked if someone was there. I requested the approval of Samuel or identification from the other side. An unknown speaker said he heard commotion on my end—not his. "Please sit in a more private place. I see you are in the living room, but all the doors are open."

Obliging, I walked upstairs. His answer was "Oh, I'm sorry, I guess the sound I'm hearing was your hard breathing that I'm attributing to noise on the line. Walking upstairs has made you pant all the more. When you sit down your breathing should improve."

Beverly (B), Unknown voice (U)

B: Correct. Who are you and what would you like to say?

U: We are here representing the people at Larry's arrival party. There is always a little anxiety connected to all returnees as to what shape they are in upon arrival. At the end Larry had sufficient medication of some sort that caused him to be pretty much "out of it" most of the way. We want you to know he arrived in good shape, but, unlike Elaine, he was not alert during the trip.

As you know, we were hoping to arrange a more interesting arrival for him. Events are never quite as we predict, so we were a little disappointed. I guess you figured that out since we didn't get back to you before now.

I know you will be glad to hear that he is recovering nicely because this transition period is important. He's not conscious yet; but we're watching him by taking turns at his bedside so that when he does gradually start awakening, he will be with somebody he recognizes right away so he won't be distressed. I just wanted you to know Larry's okay.

B: I am happy you folks are taking care of those details because he's been lonely seemingly separated from Elaine over six months.

U: Rest assured we always do. I guess that's all we wanted you to know today. As yet there have been no arrival parties, but this is a more common transition. Thank you for your prayers, your aid now in remembering Elaine, and for all those eager to catch up with him back at what we call "home".

B: Thank you for letting me know. It's a relief.

The speaker never identified himself; could have been Al, Larry's spirit guide. About five minutes later, they silently sent me a healing. I lay down for a few minutes to enjoy better breathing. How kind of them!

In Larry's next chapter we follow his activities as he sleeps, awakens, and continues his transitional period while recovering from the symbolic straight jacket worn in the life just ended.

Larry — Chapter 2

November 4, 2018

Guilty feelings of procrastination drive me to set an intention to channel Larry this morning. I have not attempted to contact Larry since his friends on the other side let me know he arrived safely and was sleeping off the effects of his July 21st transition. I know the transition phase doesn't last forever, so I had better "man up," gather my courage, and do the polite thing by asking how things have been going. Except for Kym telling me Larry had waved and shouted, "Hi, Bev" while enjoying his triathlon on the other side, I had no contact or news of him. Today, four months after Larry died, I initiate action and enquiries:

Beverly (B), Larry (L), Samuel (S)

B: Samuel, I ask for protection so Larry and I can talk freely and clearly for a frank discussion. May I talk to Larry, please?

L: [*answers immediately*] Yes, I'm here and happy you were asking about me. I recognize you have to muster up quite a lot of courage in order to talk to me. I appreciate that; and I'm sorry that is how it has worked out. However, I'm happy we are connecting now.

B: Larry, I am too. I owe you an apology that I haven't gotten to you sooner. I know you are in a state of transition and am hoping it is not too late to talk about that period. You might know that before you left the Earth, your friends from the other side had gotten together and invited me to be in on the conversation. They were planning a nice welcome-back surprise trip for you, similar to Elaine's. Unfortunately, your medications had side effects that caused you to lose consciousness, thus preventing such a remarkable return as she had.

Sorry for your missed opportunity. But for the sake of this book I'm putting together, it will be fine to have two such extremes in the same family—one mostly unconscious transition and the other with virtually everything remembered. The new book describes the transitional period from Earth to the other side. Anything you would like to contribute would be welcomed.

L: Yes, I've become aware you are writing such a book. And that you and Kym already have two books in published form. I congratulate you on those projects. I'm told they are being well received here. At this point I have not yet had the opportunity to read either of them, so I'm coming in rather blind as to what has been said and done.

My welcome here was very nice, but as you say, it was very different from the experience Elaine had, as my wife described. It's been fun for us to discuss the difference in our two trips back to this side. It will make for interesting reading for those who want to see what happens in one circumstance compared to another. I'm happy to be part of enlightening people on Earth as well as on this side regarding the wide range of things that might happen to them and their loved ones. All of that would be helpful to many. I encourage you to continue on.

Now, what would you like to know?

B: As I understand it, you went to sleep on Earth and woke up days later wherever you and Elaine are. Is that your recollection? Or did you retain snatches of what was going on?

L: I didn't have much awareness of what or where I was, nor of who was handling me. I felt I was handled gently and tenderly and was in no pain or discomfort. To me it was just a blank space because I don't know what transpired.

The first thing I remember was waking up here in something similar to a hospital bed, just as we have on Earth. There were a couple of friends around the bed as I was gradually becoming more awake and aware of my surroundings. While I remained there, one or two friends at a time stopped by my bed to welcome me back. There were no big parties with various people like Elaine had. Mine was more of a gentle adapting to life here. It was what I needed and that was fine. They assessed my needs and took care of them in advance. I don't feel cheated because once I was fully awake, we've had various parties.

Of course, I was overjoyed to see Elaine and admire how wonderful she looked and acted. It was so like meeting her for the first time. It was wonderful and made me feel good to be together again.

B: I admired that the two of you were fond of each other and affectionate as a couple. I'm pleased you are in that same state now.

How long did you stay in the hospital? Were you free to move around when you felt ready? Did you have certain obligations to fulfill before you were released on your own? Any stipulations?

L: No, but I understood you were one of the people who suggested that I be allowed to sleep as long as I felt a need. Sleep was beneficial, so I want to thank you for that. I had no idea where I was when I was asleep, even though it was not like Earth sleep. Wherever I was or whatever I was doing, I found it helpful; but I didn't have any dreams I brought back with me.

B: [*chuckle*] Well, part of my advice when asked by anyone on the other side was for selfish reasons. I didn't want to face you, so "Let Larry sleep as long as he wants" was my desire. On the other hand, because I've gone through so many phases where I couldn't sleep, I know how dreadful I feel when deprived of enough rest to replenish myself sufficiently. Maybe transitional sleep fills the same purpose. That was my honorable suggestion why they should leave you alone until you were ready to awaken on your own naturally. I'm glad you felt that time was well spent.

Do I remember correctly your spirit guide is Al?

L: Yes, that's one of them. I've got several guides; and they all help with different aspects of what I'm working on at any one time. It seems Al is with me most of the time. He's probably my main spirit guide just as Samuel is your main spirit guide. They do pretty much blend into the other. It may come quickly, but nothing is very jarring here. If there is a change of person or place, it is always a gradual, soft change. I'm feeling very secure here.

B: That's good. As for transitioning over there, are there specific things you were asked to do or process first? Were there any rules you were asked to accept? Or did you already somehow know what they were?

L: I fit in right away. I remembered a lot of friends I hadn't met in this life, but I recognized them when I moved over here. I'm pleased to be back among those friends.

B: I assume you've seen your parents, too?

L: They are well and happy to see me. [*chuckles*] Of course, they chose a body from the prime of their life like all of us do here. People seem to favor their 30s.

B: I suspect I will do the same thing, too. How do you spend your time? I got the impression that as Elaine settled in, she had the ability to choose any kind of interesting work she wanted to do. Is that how you're finding it?

L: I'm pretty much at liberty to come and go as I want. After being confined to a wheelchair and stuck in one boring room, this is wonderful to engage in various physical activities. I know eventually I will balance myself out and get a mixture of the mental and the physical, but at this point, physical stuff is really appealing to me. In the meantime, I get suggestions from my guides as to what mental exercises I might be doing.

B: [*chuckling*] Yeah, as I deteriorate in this body, I appreciate more and more just the pleasure and importance of breathing deeply, which allows me to engage in activities I want.

Well, is there some other question I should be asking about, but not aware enough yet to formulate it?

L: They tell me that you and I can make a lot of progress while one or the other of us is on the Earth plane. I've been told by Marv that he felt good about the two of you having conversations together about your marriage experience and had been able to clear away some misunderstandings. I think it would be good for us to take advantage of that ability, too.

B: Yes, Larry, I agree. I would like to clear up our situations because I have been exposed to some of our previous lives together that didn't turn out particularly happy. The more we can rid ourselves of that sour energy, the better we will all be. Maybe there is supportive prep work that can be done in sleep. But Marv tells me that we can't do the actual repair work in our sleep, it has to be on the conscious level where it originally took place.

I suggest we ask Samuel and Al what we can do and discuss, then we can start working on it.

L: They are standing right here. They can give us some initial ideas. What do you two guides think?

S: Beverly, you need to voice your fear of Larry and bravely tell him what concerns you in this life about his handling of Elaine. I suggest you do this by writing out some of the events that you remember that are so painful for you to recall.

This morning you thought of an old event that occurred while you three were waiting to go into the Eastcastle dining room for supper. It pained you greatly. So, you made an attempt to remove some of that pain from the accumulated pain you saw growing in the relationship between Elaine and Larry.

However, you, Beverly, saw the situation through your veil

and prejudices. Elaine saw the same situation through her prejudices. Larry saw the event through his life's experience. Here you all were, dealing with the separate thoughts of three people, none of whom had the same viewpoint as the others. To me that's the beginning of understanding each other's background and point of view.

Again I suggest you, Beverly, write down these events that are painful for you to experience and unpleasant for you to remember and to share.

B: That's a tough assignment because I have worked hard to forget those events. Also, is Larry aware of being part of my sorceress life?

S: No, not on the conscious level. He will be, but this is not the time. We are strictly reviewing only in the Elaine, Larry, and Beverly lives. We may not even get to previous lives for some time. Stick to this current life. If we can clear up some of that, it will be much easier on this side to take care of the earlier matters. The only reason we talked to you about the earlier lives was so you have a better, fuller understanding of what is in back of your history with Larry. At this stage while you're on Earth, I don't see any reason to go there. We've got more than enough to work with the current lives you both have shared in this current incarnation.

B: That's true! Does that sound okay, Larry?

L: Yes, I can do that.

B: Is Larry to write down some events that he remembers so we can compare notes to reach an appreciation of the other person's point of view?

S: Yeah, that's pretty much it. Whether we call in Elaine as a third party is a possibility but not a necessity at this time because neither one of you particularly have a problem being protective of Elaine. Both of you were well intentioned concerning Elaine.

B: I will start writing. I'll ask you, Samuel, to nag me about writing about the events.

S: Let's get several similar events and see what the various situations were. We may be tapping the same part of your own injured selves. In a sense we can clear them up by combining them into larger groups of similar events.

B: Back to the same pain in our relationship—I would truly like to come to a better understanding. I'm sorry, Larry, that the two of us had a stressful lifetime together. We never could seem to find a commonality. That's tough. I suppose that was all for a reason. We'll figure it out. I hope that's agreeable.

L: Yes, most definitely because I'd like to make some progress. I've been told I've got a lot of work to do.

B: You're a bright fella and a hard worker. Anything else from anybody? Thank you, folks, for the chat.

About a week later came this request:

Beverly (B), Larry (L), Samuel (S)

B: With my spirit guides permission, I would like to have a protected conversation with my brother-in-law, Larry. I have some questions to ask. Are you there, Larry?

L: Yes, but I don't know if that request for protection will pass muster. Let's give it a try and see.

B: I'm told you are still in your transitional phase. How have you changed since you arrived about four and a half months ago—physically, mentally, and spiritually?

L: I have changed in all of those ways. I don't know if I can give you specific answers to any one of those, but I know I am feeling much better about myself and about others who surround me, and that includes you, Beverly. I have spent some time thinking about you and the fact that you and I had such a difficult time arriving at a meeting of the minds during this past life. I regret very much the reaction I had to you while on Earth. I apologize for not being as helpful or creative as you would have liked me to be particularly when it came to the treatment of Elaine.

I was so concerned that by taking her off track, you might inadvertently harm her. My feelings along those lines were so intense that I couldn't see that you were simply wanting to try other healing modalities when western medical ideas weren't helping her. You wanted to see what else was out there. I'm sorry I stood so much in your way. I apology for that and wish it had not happened like that.

Apparently, that was the way it was meant to be. As I'm beginning to learn here, how we enter an earthly life becomes part of our mission in life. I guess to be closed-minded was my mission, and unfortunately, I was successful at it. Had I my druthers, I'd have thought, "Is that the best plan? Maybe we can come to some kind of an agreement."

B: Thank you, Larry. I'm touched by that and I'm sorry my reactions to you were not more direct and grown up. Perhaps that was my mission. If so, we certainly were having a conflict of missions. I will be happy to talk about that in depth at a later time.

I'm going to try to stick to today's list of written down, succinct questions. The next one is: do you have any form of classes you have to attend? If so, who are your teachers and what are your subjects?

L: No, at this stage, I'm not required to do any kind of school work. I am at liberty to spend my time any way I want to. I'm aware that this transitional time period is limited, so I'm making the best use of it that I can. I'm getting in all the fun things I can that were missed during the years I was not at all agile or available to have fun. I'm catching up on my fun quota now. I will not do any classes until they say, "Okay, move on, you've had your transition." I will meet that with mixed emotions because I am having fun, but I know there is a seriousness that needs to be tackled here, too.

B: Well, enjoy it. Do you grieve anything from this past life? I mean grieve in all seriousness. What can you do to help yourself work your way through grief now? What methods or techniques are you learning?

L: Yes, there are things I miss; and I am sad. I'm sad I didn't diligently take time to find and contact my ancestors and pass down the family history and photographs, which you have now taken on as a task. Yet, it's using up the time that you need to be spending on your projects. So, maybe I can make some kind of a deal with you. Maybe I can do my best to help you find places to pass on your things in lieu of doing my family memorabilia—some kind of a swap.

I do grieve sometimes, not heavily like people grieve on Earth, but there is a sadness to know that while life was a story I participated in and had a good time learning about, it's suddenly over. Elaine showed me, when she sent the message to you about you walking through Eastcastle for the last time, how everything just shut down. Poof and it was gone. It was the same thing I got on this side. It is gone; and I really can't return back to it. Yeah, I can have memories and visit with friends who shared it with me, but as far as participating in it or adding new parts to it. No.

I can't say I am without grief because I have experienced it. It's there; I recognize the signs. I don't know if there is anything that can be done about grief. Knowing you have to work your way through grief will help people who are going to read your books if they are open to that idea. Enjoy the good parts of your earthly life because when it's gone, it is *really* gone.

B: I sense Elaine goes through grief sometimes when she talks to me. There were times when she walked away from our conversations as they were winding down. She was exhibiting signs of grief and had to pull away. I'm guessing not everyone feels it to the same degree.

L: Yes, I would say that is true.

B: What do you look forward to now?

L: I'm going to have to wait and see what is in store for me. I am not aware of past lives. The only thing I have now is the memory of this life as Larry, so I'm talking blind at this stage. I trust my guides to introduce things when it is most beneficial to know about them and deal with them. That's the wonderful aspect of having these guides to help us accept or be aware of our pasts and help us work our way through them.

Each and every one of us has done things we don't want to think about. Yet, it's like our energy is stored in various places in our bodies. Somehow that unpleasant stuff has to be dug out and moved. The guides see the master plan and figure out when to face things. They've got the keys to the books that tell us our history.

S: In your case, Beverly, I suggest you see your unresolved resentment issues being neatly packaged. Visualize a man called Max, your internal maintenance man, stacking those resentment boxes one on top of another in your body's closet. He's the one who has to deal with your angry thought energies that should have been *immediately* tossed out when they were experienced, not packaged and stored. That negative energy doesn't belong in your body. Max is doing yeoman's work setting the boxes around your body, trying to protect you from the concentrated damage your thoughts are creating. Unfortunately, he's overwhelmed. Your packages are arriving faster than he can jettison them, so he has to keep storing them somewhere.

This behavior still goes on today. You have no idea how intensely your brain gets you in trouble because it wanders off into areas it has no business thinking about. It is to your detriment. You "brainiac" people are the ones who have the most trouble freeing yourselves of negative thought energy.

Your *motive* for holding on to your opinions doesn't matter. It's what gets stuck in your body that counts. Because an idea gets stuck, it thinks it belongs there! The idea thinks it was put there after careful consideration. But energy is energy; and it doesn't have feelings. That's the part that's so hard for Earth people to understand. It's the excitement of the energy that Earth people get caught up in whereas the energy itself has no emotions. The misplaced energy does all the damage; the storage of that energy is destructive to our bodies.

B: I appreciate both of you talking to me candidly because your words touch my heart. Too bad, Larry, we never set more time together to speak heart to heart. Our lives might have been more internally serene.

Is there anything else you would like to introduce?

L: I realize I was obstructing you from having a close relationship with your sister Elaine. I apologize for that. At this stage I am even recognizing how selfish I was in demanding her time, which was unfair to you. I could have made life easier for you because you needed a friend in many stages in your life, but I felt Elaine was not in the best position to help you. I am regretful of that. Do you accept my apology?

B: Yes, Larry, I do because you and I have both made a lot of judgments and decisions we both wish we hadn't made. I do accept it and gladly give you my apologies, too.

L: I thank you for your kindness to me. I do receive prayers from you and appreciate how helpful they are to me at this stage. Like Elaine, I had no idea how important prayer was and what pleasant things can happen with the energy that is sent to us.

In all of the books you write, please tell people to take prayer seriously and use it judiciously and thoughtfully because we on this side really relish the contact with people on the Earth—particularly high-minded, helpful energy. We need lots of that just as Earth people need lots of that same energy—not that we are in competition for the same energy. It's important that we keep recycling that good stuff. I think that's important for people to know.

When I come out of this transitional period, hopefully we will have time while you are still on Earth because it will help us greatly when you are back here. I'm all for speeding things along by speaking this way.

B: Thank you—and thank you, Samuel.

❋ ❋ ❋

In the next chapter, much to my chagrin, you'll see examples of how the best laid plans can get off course by our buried flaws when our goal is celebration of tasks completed successfully. Perhaps we really don't respect what the purpose of life on Earth is. Maybe our views are still too small.

Larry  Chapter 3

August 14, 2018

The crematorium mailed Larry's ashes to me at my home. Now I have to plan my final job for Elaine and Larry. I emailed an announcement to the pastor so she could inform the friends of Elaine and Larry where their remains will be placed. She thought it would bring comfort and a sense of closure to all:

> Pastor,
>
> I want you and others to know that I am making arrangements with my former minister, Herb, to prepare a service for us to spread the ashes of Elaine and Larry in Cincinnati in the near future. As requested by Larry, I will spread their ashes on my two acre property where years ago I planted a few native trees on the gentle western slope. I used to mow all the grass back there, but now I only mow a winding path through the assortment of grasses and wildflowers because they are so pretty.
>
> I believe the family of deer will approve. In the twilight I often see the deer resting on the rise of the hill where they feel safe as night approaches. Come morning I can spot the matted grass in the individual locations in which they have rested. Over the years I have seen furry-eared fox, raccoons, and woodchucks enjoying life there. It's a lovely spot for Elaine and Larry to become part of them.
>
> Beverly

September 29, 2018 email to the family's pastor:

Pastor,

I will not be attending Larry's memorial in Milwaukee. I had hoped my unpredictable bouts of dizziness would end by now, but I need to stay local rather than try to travel. Therefore, I will join your group in quiet meditation during that time here at home. Feel free to read my earlier email about spreading Elaine and Larry's ashes.

I just asked Kym to look in on both Elaine and Larry. She said Elaine was happily studying in a classroom and Larry was about to enter a canoe race but stopped on the beach to run to the water's edge to wave and shout, "Hello, Bev." I suspect a race is Larry's version of being happy to be out of a wheelchair—like Elaine wanted to dance! So, both are well.

Beverly

❋ ❋ ❋

October 7, 2018

Kym and I had agreed the service to spread the ashes of Elaine and Larry would begin after I returned home from Sunday morning Unity church service and grabbed a quick lunch. The weather being unusually hot and humid, I felt drained of energy by the time I got home, wishing I had switched the service to yesterday because that was a glorious autumnal day. The idea crossed my mind to cancel today's event and reschedule it because sitting outside in the blazing heat had little appeal. However, the afternoon had been set aside for not only Kym and me in the body, but also for spirits on the other side. So we decided to stick with the original plan.

In the cooler comfort of the house, Kym and I reviewed our plans so there would be no slip-ups to the dignity of the service before we headed outside. First, I would channel Rev. Herb's comments, which would be recorded. Next, both sets of ashes would be spread under the sycamore tree I had planted decades ago at the rear of my property connected to a wooded area.

But the afternoon didn't go smoothly. The end result was two uncomfortable women. One seated in a wobbly, canvas chair; the other seated on the ground surrounded by hungry insects.

Prior to setting this date, there were several long discussions with the other side about combining this service with the release of some baggage from our respective lives as Elaine, Larry, and myself as well as baggage from our shared, past, intertwined lives revolving around the sorceress. Hence, we three would each be releasing our own baggage from two different eras in history.

I became increasingly nervous about attempting that goal for the simple reason that I didn't think we were at the same developmental stage. For example, Larry would not yet be ready to deal with these past lives as it related to me because some unpleasant information was being withheld from him at this stage. It seemed unfair to rush him.

Next was the question of my ability to channel clearly. I was having trouble. Who would take over if I fumbled the ball? I wanted to channel and the other side wanted me to channel, but could I? So here we were at that critical moment. Show time!

Things did not go well when I tried to start channeling Reverend Herb's talk. Something was amiss. The tone started fine but quickly became increasingly negative. Kym agreed, "That doesn't sound like Herb. I've never known him to be gloomy before." I felt the same way. Believing a hacker had caught me off guard, I stopped. I had failed. Unfortunately, that happens, and I have to deal with disappointment when it comes and not let it throw me for a loop, but it upset me. Kym had to step in.

What follows is the core of the Spreading of Ashes service recording as channeled:

Art (A), Beverly (B), Elaine (E), Herb (H), Kym (K), Larry (L)

K: Today we celebrate Elaine and Larry who passed this year. I'm going to channel Herb, Elaine, Larry, and anyone else in this crowd of friend and family spirits who want to speak. Herb, as minister, I will give you the floor.

H: We are here today to complete the circle of life for the souls of Elaine and Larry. This is a rite of passage for both of them for a job well done. The current incarnation of Elaine and Larry has been started; and the first leg of their journeys has been completed. Wonderful celebrations of their work have occurred with all of the people they love. Both have already begun moving into the next phase of their journey.

In this recent life, Larry wanted to experience what it was like to be loved. He came in as a character who wasn't always easy to be loved. He had many difficulties in that area, but he comes forward to say he felt loved here even though he didn't always behave like he wanted love. Here, his opportunities meant, *How could he be loved without acting lovable?* He has accomplished it because he was well loved by Elaine, his family, and other people, including Beverly who realized later in life that she loved him too.

L: I thank everyone in attendance who have been on Earth with me in this recent incarnation. I had the most wonderful wife and a wonderful life. As we all know, the journey is not over, just the first leg of the race is finished. I was happy to end it because I wanted to join my Elaine.

K: I see them both very young with Elaine next to him holding his hand with her head on his arm saying, "You loved me; and I loved you. I've been waiting for you."

E: I also wanted the experience of love, but I wanted to know if I could love myself. The love from Beverly and my parents proved I was lovable. Taking and trusting their lead, I found my own self-love. Sister, you made it easy for me to be loved and to find my own love, because you loved me so much—and, of course, so did our parents.

Beverly, because you're the last family member on Earth, you get the main focus. [*giggles*] I wish you knew and believed that as much as you admired me and put me on a pedestal, I did the same for you. You had struggles I never had, you had to go through things I never did, and you came through it so well.

H: You sisters were both very different women on different journeys. Yet, you always stayed together and helped each other even after Elaine could no longer communicate with you, Beverly, but she never took you for granted. She always loved to see you as much as you loved to see her.

We're going to bless this ground, this land, this location to hold the last earthly snippets of these two amazing, courageous souls who journeyed down in this time and space to experience the wonders of the Earth plane. It's an appropriate place to be since it is tied to two other members of the family, Uncle Arthur and Beverly who each in turn have owned this house and property. Now the four of you walk this land in spirit. It's a beautiful resting place. [*everybody chimed in*]

A: [*Uncle Art stepped forward*] I'm honored that you have chosen as a final resting space this property that is so loved. We owe it all to Larry who suggested that he and his wife would like to be on this land for he understood the location's peaceful charm.

K: Let us begin by spreading Larry's ashes around the sycamore tree.

At this point in the service, Kym handed me the recorder and said, "Bev, talk about your fond memories of Larry." She then picked up his heavy bag and began at the trunk of the tree to release Larry's ashes in a spiral around the tree trunk.

Kym didn't realize what a trigger Larry was for my anger. There were no fond memories! Instead, I went into a complete meltdown and insisted I take over the job of spreading the ashes around the sycamore. I telepathically called Larry a lifelong, lousy friend to Elaine because he consistently stifled her. Dealing with Larry was always a tense, unpleasant relationship for me. Now, only now, finally all kinds of brutally honest words and thoughts flowed out of me as his ashes powdered the grasses at my feet.

When it was time for Elaine's ashes, I spent endless numbers of spirals around the tree apologizing to her for my rude thoughts and anger toward Larry on their day of celebration. I hated myself for the pain I caused them—and Kym, who saved the day unaware of my internal temper tantrum. With the conclusion of distributing the ashes and the service, I asked Kym to leave me so I could be alone on the hill. Actually, I wanted to hide in shame.

The little bit of solace I could find was remembering Samuel's words after Elaine's memorial service in Milwaukee months earlier, "Everybody finds what they need to find at these occasions." This service was no different. Today Kym saw only a tribute to two lives. I found a path to release boxed up anger and to take the first steps of my grief being released. Those on the other side in attendance must find their own answers.

❄ ❄ ❄

October 8, 2018, Monday evening when I was alone in my room, I telepathically heard a voice introduce himself the way I prefer—without mystery:

Beverly (B), Herb (H)

H: I was the minister at yesterday's service in your backyard. My name is Herbert, otherwise known as Hal in your first two books. May we talk about yesterday's event? I'm anxious to know how you are feeling today about the procedure.

B: [*pleased to hear him*] Yes, I definitely welcome your visit, Bosom Buddy. As you prepared the service, were you able to interview both Elaine and Larry beforehand?

H: Yes, we went over their experiences very thoroughly.

B: Yes, I figured as much. You were always one to be well researched and organized, which people always appreciated. I, on the other hand, was flustered and quite disturbed as you could obviously see.

H: Would you tell me what in particular upset you? I come wanting to know about the way you were feeling concerning the service itself. Were you satisfied?

B: Your comments were succinct, interesting, and on target. You summed up why Elaine and Larry came together, i.e., what their missions were for this lifetime. Frankly, I was stunned by their life themes, but your explanations made sense. You described what their challenges were and the fact that they both succeeded in their missions. Therefore, they are ready to move on in their journey. Am I understanding that correctly?

H: Yes. However, I wanted to let you know I was also upset, but not so much by what you were going through. We ministers find angry reactions like yours are rather typical of people with a lot of unfinished business with the newly departed. That did not surprise me at all because I was familiar with the level of your frustration with your brother-in-law's control issues.

What did disappoint me was the fact that so much time was spent on production details like where to put the ashes, how to arrange them, where people should sit—maintenance stuff!

B: As for placement of the ashes, I'm aware some people feel comforted by some symbol attached to how the ashes are placed. I'm not one of them because it seems like a distraction. But if it's important to another's peace of mind, I'll probably oblige.

Yes, I had lingering anxiety over having lost all control over the event, starting in the planning stages and ending with my display of anger. True. I was unpolished, which detracted from the important purpose of Elaine and Larry having successfully reached a milestone.

H: People on this side definitely noticed the confused informality coming from the Earth side activities.

B: Does that disturb you?

H: No, but looking at the broader scope, I thought because of your connection to these folks, you ought to know what their reactions were. As far as the human condition of you coping with a humid day, I think that escaped most spirits because by the time they are over here for a while, they forget how humidity affects the physical body and its temperament. Don't worry about that.

B: It sounds to me that most of your folks were more interested in the performance instead of the contents of the service.

H: [*emphatically*] Exactly! That's my point! People weren't thinking about the important aspect of what these two people have accomplished by the end of their lifetime, which was what we wanted to concentrate on. Your friends could see, as we looked over the people assembled, that they were not catching the significance of the service. We got frustrated. Consequently, we were unwittingly expressing that frustration to you, which added to your anxiety energetically. We didn't want to make a downer of it for you—that was just our emotional reaction to what we were witnessing at the moment on site.

The frequent topic you and we share has to do with questioning if everybody realizes they've still got work to do even after death. Many spirits feel, since they are dead, they are already in heaven with no need to work—without realizing that this space is also part of the illusion.

Actually, our goal is to move forward, to learn more, to spread more love, and accumulate more love. That's why we are finding your books are successful here—partly because spirits here have the added benefit of access to past life records if they choose to reach out and learn from them.

I think the answer you are wanting from us is whether or not to talk about this topic in this transition book. To be perfectly honest, yes, we think people on Earth should be aware of the fact that the learning process continues.

This is not the ultimate heaven they have imagined from the stories of uninformed religious leaders. However, this is the next step. Samuel and I don't have any objection to you saying that kind of statement in the book. We don't want you to overwhelm people with that unpleasant thought, but perceptive readers will catch on. It will light a fire in them that says, "Hey, I never thought of this as just being the next step of growing into companionship with God, which is the ultimate goal of the journey."

You and Kym are probably becoming aware that much of your audience is equally uninformed of what life is all about, even once they are on this side. You see how important clarity is. Yes, we're doing great scientific work here, but as far as attitude changes—it ain't happening. Those of us working on increasing spiritual awareness get discouraged about our slow progress. Anyway, I thought I'd consciously let you know what we are dealing with on this side, too.

B: What would you advise me? How can I help you?

H: Here's my reality check. Whatever problems in your work you are dealing with on Earth, you will be dealing with it on this side, too. I suspect you have become suspicious of the new aspects of your work. Yes, you are officially unaware that you are leaving your body and teaching in small, night classes up here to people on this side who are ready to consider what you are suggesting in your books.

B: Somehow, I'm not surprised to hear I am doing another form of night work these days. My buddies up there never seem to miss a teaching opportunity. I was suspicious you were giving me audience feedback for my purpose as a teacher.

Another concern of mine was my complete meltdown over Larry yesterday. Some of my night pupils might have been in the audience yesterday and seen me demonstrate how the grieving process might play out—how embarrassing.

H: We were not surprised you had an emotional response when you were away from the recorder. Of course, we knew, as did you, it was not really alone-time because those in attendance could see you were angry. It was a good experience for those who were able to understand that you were releasing the anger. It was the place to do it. The relief is not over, but it is a start for your grieving process. We were not shaken; we were not upset that you had a bit of a meltdown.

B: I sincerely know I love Larry because of the depth of my emotion. I don't know where that love comes from, for it did not originate in this Beverly life. Still, I would like to get rid of those negative feelings I have right now. I want to apologize for what I said to him, yet I know it was my Beverly truth.

H: That can wait for later. In fact, you did extend your thoughts backward onto a previous life when Larry and Elaine along with Marvin were interwoven in your sorceress life. All of that has got to be untwisted, corrected and dealt with, which is what we had hoped to do in this service when we discussed the pros and cons of healing past lives where we saw a connection with the recent past. In fact, it was during the discussion period for yesterday's service that Elaine told you she was your elder daughter[1] when she died by your hand when you were the sorceress. Unfortunately, recognition came up in your mind. We thought that might happen because you had collected enough facts to know what resulted. I'll just leave it; we'll get to that eventually.

B: Elaine's comment about me, she put so succinctly. We had a wonderful, though long-distance, friendship to support each other. I'm grateful for both of us responding to each other's needs when noticed. To me, that lifted my spirits greatly. I'm so thankful for her as my sister and the daughter I [*gulping*] ... We'll have to work on that one day, too.

H: I can't talk about that. I'd like to, but I'm not permitted. Again, there will come a time. So, I guess that's all I really had to say.

B: I'm grateful for you contacting me.

H: Thank you, my dear. I'll see you "in the trenches."

I feel better after my talk with Herb, but it never occurred to me that a sad mood generated by the people on the other side can serve to influence us on Earth. In this case, Herb's disappointment in his congregation helped spread sadness in the backyard.

---

1   See an earlier conversation between Elaine and Beverly on page *205*

This event for Elaine and Larry was an important celebration of diligence. But, my conduct removed any dignity I had wished to confer on them for their successes. I realize I had spent too little time thinking of this as a rite of passage for them. Yet, I knew it was a powerful ending for me. In hindsight counseling would have helped me; I needed outside prep time to handle my issues that were bound to be confronted at this event.

All things considered, I am not particularly pleased with myself today. Unfortunately, there are no do-overs here. I'm assuming other humans are blindly taking on this task even more unprepared than I was—just a thought that might have merit for others.

❋ ❋ ❋

Others struggled, too, with the loss of Larry and Elaine. Here's an excerpt from an email from the family's pastor:

October 17, 2018

> Beverly,
>
> I was judgmental toward Larry, especially after they moved to Eastcastle and Elaine's Parkinson's got worse. I didn't make peace with Larry until the July day before he became unresponsive. He wanted me to tell him more about Elaine that he had forgotten; he hung on my every word. The next day as I sat by his bed, I realized that I cared deeply for him[2]; and I had peace. It was a struggle, but I know I cared deeply for both Elaine and Larry.
>
> Pastor

October 19, 2018, email to the pastor:

> Pastor,
>
> Thanks for writing. Maybe a bit of background might help you.
>
> When Elaine graduated from the five-year engineering program, getting a job was not easy. Luckily, Falk was a

---

[2] This is an example of Larry's life theme. He wasn't lovable to the pastor, yet she was able to love him.

small local company that was willing to hire her. Almost immediately work stress put her in a meltdown and forced her into bed for a time. I remember how mother worried about her career choice. Fortunately, Elaine rallied and after a delayed start became Falk's first lady engineer.

Elaine also went through the same stress as many newlyweds. Larry assumed the conservative, 1960s male attitude of "Sure, you can work a 40-hour-a-week job if it amuses you, but women's real work is doing the washing, ironing, and cooking." Elaine ended up in bed exhausted and contemplating a divorce. To Larry's credit, he saw they needed help and agreed to extensive marriage counseling. Fortunately they found a wise woman who was able to guide Larry into sharing the household responsibilities. I admired him greatly for seeing the inequity of the new marital mode as he really pitched in with the mundane tasks.

However, he never got the hang of letting her express her thoughts or decisions, but she made it work. As she grew weaker after retirement, Larry got more frustrated and acted like she was being a naughty child because she couldn't make her feet move. More than once I complained to her that I thought Larry was a Male Chauvinistic Pig (MCP, as they were called then). Pastor, you were not the only one expressing your opinion to Elaine. She knew and could see for herself, but was always loyal to him.

At Eastcastle he became more vocal; and I was often embarrassed for them in the public dining room when he berated her. If I gave a look or said anything, he viewed me as one butting into his marriage. So it was a relief for Elaine and I to go away together to Lake Geneva. There we had peace and fun plus she could eat at her own pace. Unfortunately, by this time in their lives, Larry was no longer in a mood to get counseling and Elaine's physical needs were intensified. I was so worried about how Elaine was feeling about herself. She couldn't or wouldn't speak about such personal things in life with me.

I take comfort now in knowing I was seeing Larry through *my* tender Beverly lens. What I was finding hurtful, Elaine was seeing as a challenge to be faced. I was coming in at various times (as I assume you were also) to give her courage to go on and have the best life she could.

Pastor, I'm happy to know you found peace and love for Larry at the end. You and I might have had similar unconscious insights of remembering him from a happier life and could recognize the pre-existing love we had for him. That's why when spreading his ashes, I was sad— because I was pulling forward my anger, not my love.

One day we will know the answers.

Love,

Bev

❈ ❈ ❈

July 16, 2018, a conversation between Beverly as the Sorceress and Elaine as the Sorceress' daughter

E: First, let me say, Beverly, that in the previous life we shared, I was one of the daughters that you had when you were the sorceress during the unfortunate circumstances that led to my dying under your hand at that time. I'm sorry to let you know that so early in this phase of my current relationship with you in spirit form. I was hoping to keep that private a little bit longer. I knew you had been wondering about the sorceress' two daughters and concerned about what ever happened to them. I knew your heart was in the right place about their whereabouts.

Yes, it is true I was your older girl, but even so, I don't have a lot of memory about that time. I haven't been here long enough to warrant getting a lot of those details. When that time comes, I will know more, but now it all seems rather vague. Marvin, your beloved baby during that life, doesn't remember much either. I'm kinda in that same position. Maybe it's just a matter of the guides temporarily cloaking us from becoming overloaded on past lives when we need to concentrate on the life we just completed. Whatever the guides think wise is fine. But, yes, that did happen.

B: [*slumping*] Oh, my heart just sank. What can a person say? I know so little about that event myself. I'm terribly sorry this happened and life came to such a sad end for us. [*crying*] I'm sorry I inflicted such pain on you and prevented you from the chance of a productive, helpful life.

As I think of it now, isn't it ironic that we automatically assumed that the boy was the child who was going to save us? [*chuckling*] We never even considered it could be one of the girls who were going to save us from castle intrigues? Forgive me if I sound flippant. I'm not, but that's what struck me right now.

E: Funny you should mention that, but that thought occurred to me, too. I guess we are a couple of woman libbers ahead of our time. And your apology is accepted because I probably knew in advance what was being asked of me when I signed on to the eldest daughter job. So it must have suited my purposes and went according to plan. We'll just leave it at that.

Bev, I hear you complaining a lot about the system in which we go into a life consciously blind as to what to expect and what our job is. I can understand how you feel. I felt that way too. I must say I've become much more open toward the system as it's established here. I know you are thinking of Jim Jones and his followers drinking the Kool Aid, but I don't think that is applicable because that doesn't seem to fit either. I guess you just have to view it from this side and forget what your earthly thoughts are.

B: I feel something on my head right now. I don't know what it is.

E: Well, I think it's somebody from this side stroking your head trying to comfort you. Yeah, it's okay, you'll get over this idiosyncrasy. Try to lighten up because we're getting tired of hearing you complain about it. [*laughter*]

B: And I'm getting tired of saying it, so I'll do my best to call a truce and keep mum! Love you.

With the celebration of the completion of a portion of their journeys, Elaine and Larry meld into the population. The following epilogue serves as a reminder, as Reverend Herb reflected in the last chapter, of how we influence each other from both sides of the veil. We are inevitably linked and might be wise to cultivate these friendships carefully.

Epilogue

The goal of the other side: Once the transition period is over and you are rested and ready to carry on in your journey, do your best to take the wide view and bring forth the best in yourself and others as you travel onward.

Spring 2019, Nancy

Beverly (B), Nancy (N)

B: Nancy, do you have a message to put in the epilogue?

N: Beverly, I'm pleased you have persevered with creating this transition book. I'm honored to be a part of it, but I'm eager for you to finish because there are so many other things I want you to do before you decide it's time to leave the Earth plane.

As my parting shot, please get the world or society to know we've got plenty of work to be done on this side of the veil just as you do on that side. The work is similar and leads to making life better for every single one of us. Let people know how important their input is—no matter what side of the veil they are on.

I'm still enjoying life on this side. Myself, I'm busy working to help people adjust to situations when they arrive here in bad shape from their hell. You have named our group soothers, which pretty much sums it up. I do my best to help troubled ones ease into a better view of their life and its importance. My work is gratifying, so I'm happy to do it.

Being able to meet so many people, my world has expanded greatly. Some folks were intimately associated with me; others I'm newly beginning to meet and appreciate. To summarize how things are for me now, it seems no matter where I am, I'm happy when people find something interesting and important to do.

Even though by Earth time it has been several years since I made my transition, the topic of your book, that period was helpful. The fact that I could work at my own pace was appreciated and a marvelous experience. I was neither rushed nor slowed down. I hope others, when the time comes, would have an attitude of being receptive, being open to ideas, and looking for opportunities presented to them on this side.

My love and regards to all, friend and stranger. It's important to remember we are all in this together to help each other. Thank you for asking me for a comment.

Your friend,

Nancy

B: Oh, I love you and wish we had known each other longer in this life.

N: Yeah. Me too, but we've got more to come, so never fear. We will enjoy what's coming next, too.

Spring 2019, Joshua

Beverly (B), Joshua (J), Samuel (S)

B: Josh, would you like to make a contribution to the epilogue of the transition book?

J: I'm pleased you are getting back with me because I think you have gotten the pertinent happenings in a logical progression so that readers can follow the events in my life. However, there was more that I wanted to convey, what did not get the proper attention earlier—or perhaps I didn't know well enough at the time we talked. So, I would like to make three additions.

First, why are you always putting me in the role of a victim? I think people need to understand that was the life I *chose* to lead. I took on the role of being the victim; my attitude set the tone that I put on myself. In truth, the opportunity to live and comprehend life from a handicapped position was what I chose to do of my own free will. It was not something thrust on me; it was my adventuresomeness that said, "I don't know enough about this topic, so I'm gonna go into Earth and live this experience. So I did. [*chuckle*] Well, it wasn't "Oh, poor Josh." Poor Josh chose to do this!

As I look back at one of the live conversations you and I had during a church potluck dinner, I think you were gently wanting to lead me into thinking, "As an adult, I should be figuring, *Well, I'm getting to that age where most people can no longer physically do the sports I am still yearning to do. Realistically, if I were able bodied now, how many more years would I have the ability to play rigorous sports? All bodies approach the age of rebellion eventually.*" I did not want to hear your message nor was I mentally prepared to make that shift in thinking. Now I understand that was something you learned from your sister, the dancer.

B: Yes. I recall a conversation when Elaine and I, in our fifties, talked with a ballet dancer, in his thirties, who lamented noticing the decline in his athletic abilities and worried how he was going to support himself while remaining in the field he loved. Later, Elaine's private comment to me was, "What did he expect? We know how punishing ballet is on the body. He feels the pain in his own body and sees it in his fellow dancers. What did he think he was going to do with his life when his body reached that stage and couldn't professionally hack it any longer?" She was right. That's when I realized what a tough-minded, realistic cookie Elaine was!

J: That was perceptive of your sister. Your body takes you to various levels of abilities, but once that time frame is over, you gotta be prepared enough for the next adventure to make a success of life in that new spot. Even if I hadn't fallen out of that tree and hurt myself, I did not realize there was a time limit for playing all the sports I loved playing. I kidded myself by refusing to catch onto that piece of wisdom. It was part of my learning process, but I didn't keep my eye on the ball in terms of what was coming next. How was I going to adjust to my handicap so I am productive in the next stage of my life? I got tied up in self pity and not wanting to move into the next phase. My mentioning this might help a reader who is stuck like I was.

B: Yes, your insights in this book are appreciated. That reminds me, many times I've tried to figure out your death experience in which you believed you were trapped in a deep abyss of endless darkness. The abyss turned out to be a bubble through which you could not see, yet some kind of guardians were able to keep tabs on you—probably waiting for someone like me to come by. Were you building a hell for yourself?

J: Well, I've wondered about that, too. I might have been in the early stages of wanting to shut myself off and was successfully doing it. So far as I could see, I was in complete darkness in a huge space from which I saw no way out. I suspect, as you have, I might unknowingly have been starting to build a hell for myself.

B: [*having doubts*] Now I, Beverly, am sitting here thinking, "Am I inventing this? Am I blank enough to hear clearly Josh on the other side?"

S: You *are* blank enough; and he is giving you his honest reaction as he thinks back to what was going on. So I would stick with what you wrote. In his life, Josh will always return back to this period and question himself on what was really going on. Self-reflection is an important aspect to inform the reader. Like you, Beverly, you don't look at one experience and think now I've got it, because the next time you go back to that event and question it, often more is revealed. It's a matter of layering up answers until you get a fuller picture as time goes on. That's the way it's been designed.

B: Yes, getting the broad view first always helps me appreciate the subtle details when they come. It's a gentle way to process life as it unfolds before us. Now if I can return to Josh, is there anything else you would like to add to the epilogue?

J: I'm pleased that I have this wonderful connection with my mom now. Between us, she on the Earth and me on the other side, we have this ability to talk with each other and develop our relationship in a deeply satisfactory way. Yes, it would have been nice to have this closeness while I was on Earth. It would have made her life easier, but we can do it now even though we are on different planes. It's wonderful that this chance is there and that she and I are taking full use of that opportunity.

I encourage people who feel they have unfinished business with someone on the other side to think there is no reason to stop working on that relationship. Just work on it! It is so much easier and better now than if mother and I had said, "Well, I guess with my death that's over and done with because we can't do a lot about it." I am grateful that she is aware and for us to be establishing such a close bond with each other. I thank you, Beverly, and Kym for her help too. I wish you all the best. Bye for now.

Spring 2019, Marvin

Beverly (B), Marvin (M)

B: Let's see if I have the energy to do a third channeled conversation this morning. Marv, why don't we give it a try. I'm anxious to know how things are going with you. Do you have some comments to add to the epilogue?

M: Yes, I do. I'm glad we are continuing our conversation. I have been thinking about your request and have a couple of items I'd like to include.

B: Okay. What would you like to say?

M: I want the world to know there was a misunderstanding between us when we married. We were very far apart and we got further apart during the actual marriage. At the time of the wedding, we assumed we knew each other very well because we came from the same neighborhood, school, and friends. Plus we knew each other over a long period of years. But, we hadn't realized how different we were until it came time to live together. That surprise was painful to both of us as we realized how much our opinions differed with each other.

[*uncomfortable pause*] I'm trying to keep it positive.

B: Yes, I sense that you are struggling.

M: I don't want any harmful influences to come particularly at this time in my education when I'm trying to reset my pattern of thinking. What positive aspects can we employ to help each other?

Not make any mistakes in the first place—[*laughs*] Fat chance of that!

Get rid of lingering, repetitive problems before they become massive obstacles.

B: That's ideal, but that's tough, too. Recently, I'm told you've been busy recommending some practical advice to folks on the your side. Do you know what I'm referring to?

M: Yes, I told Larry, our brother-in-law, that he could have direct conversation with you on Earth even though he was on this side—just like you and I have been able to initiate discussions of our own earthly experiences. It appears this opportunity is not widely understood by all spirits.

Later, by chance, I ran into a young, deceased woman here who longed to communicate with her intuitive mom on Earth. I suggested she make a serious concentrated effort to connect because it would be beneficial to both of them. Progress can still be made in their relationship. Even if her mom wasn't intuitive, the connection could be established through a talented medium.

B: Coincidentally, though unaware of Marvin's and my conversation, Kym was in a new client session when she was interrupted by the surprise appearance of this same young woman who said she met Marv, and he told her about the ability to talk to her mom. He also mentioned to her about Kym as a medium and her helpfulness in this type of connection. The daughter had prompted her mom to hunt Kym down. The point here being that it is amazing the help offered us from both sides of the veil.

I appreciate you telling various people on your side, Marv, of our experience of talking to each other from our different planes. I'm grateful this communication ability has helped us and will, in turn, assist them if desired.

M: Bev, I've still got a lot of anger I haven't worked though any more than you have. Between the two of us, we've got a lot of stored resentments; and that stuff is really stubborn. I encourage you to get a real scrub brush and get rid of that stuff, because I love you. That infection is soaked in and the stain is hard to scrub out on this side. It is something to be taken seriously.

I'm sure you remember Steve, my grade school chum, who would say I had a chip on my shoulder. I sure did because everyone could see it in my facial expression. That chip was there; and how weighty it was! I encourage anyone who has that problem to work hard to find what the source of that anger is and how to get rid of it ASAP.

You and I are at the very beginnings of repair. The fact that we are tangled up in more than one lifetime doubles the need and complexity. On the other hand, once we get a handle on it, resentment will go POOF. I've seen it happen to other people. They need to get a firm handle on the problem. Then they go to all the sources where their complicated lives are interwoven around each other. Once that is sorted out, there is a massive relief as the stressful traits that they were lugging around seem to disappear. I do anticipate you and I will be able to continue working at this. Yes, it's better not to have it at all. But, my words of encouragement are: knock the problem off at the bud before it blossoms.

It's good to talk to you, my dear. (*I think both of us said that.*)

❋ ❋ ❋

Spring 2019, Elaine

Beverly (B), Elaine (E)

B: [*kidding*] What insightful, inventive closing thoughts does my sister have to offer us?

E: [*chuckling*] The thing about the Earth that you don't appreciate is how glad you are to be here on the other side without conflict. You need to realize in a conflict-free area, without that kind of stimulation and manufactured enemy, you can slip into the most mundane things imaginable. So, before you cross over, it's not a bad idea to think of things you'd like to do on the other side if your guide thinks it's got something to help in the grand scope of things.

Everything is fine—we make things happen, but this is not normal Earth life. On Earth folks get used to winning some and losing some. Here, most of that hard edge is missed. So in designing their next life, if people are not careful, they forget how devastating a physical life can be if they are careless. Some of the events they plan to confront are tough.

Depend on the alertness of your spirit guides who can help you face the reality of some of these situations. If too much hardship slips in through your free will, it is a disservice to the people trying to guide you. It's true that without challenges, you lose your mental edge. Yet, letting you face too big a challenge in the next life is not desired. Challenges are not bad things unless they are way out of scale.

It's important, once you arrive here and are fairly well acclimated, you select different jobs that keep you anchored in the broad view. When you are living in comfortable conditions, it's easy to forget others who are not as lucky. Here you can reach out and stay connected to Earth's residents, many of whom are living in miserable conditions you can help lighten.

B: What are you're telling me?

E: My point is, people are apt to think *this* is heaven as their Earth churches have been telling them. We don't have streets of gold, of course, but it's very pleasant living here. They think death is its own reward—no more work. Actually there are helpful projects here to do, which will raise all of us up as a society.

Smart people remember the past and come prepared, knowing they need to have a project or two. My observation is people on this side have more than enough time to volunteer to be listeners—to be connected to people on Earth or wherever they might be able, or want, to connect. So I'm advocating a whole network of people with volunteer jobs who will help raise the energy of the whole universe by helping people develop the best within themselves.

B: A contemporary version of pen-pals has wonderful possibilities. Your thoughts have opened up new areas of exploration in my brain. Getting rid of my negative hang ups that are dragging me down by engaging in something joyously beneficial would be a step in the right direction for the spiritual mindset of me and others in the community.

I'm curious, when you officially came out of your transition phase, you decided to look for a job and had several interviews. Have you taken a permanent job?

E: Well, I have taken a job; and as it turns out, I am to help you with this transition book more than I had thought. I am happy to do it because I see the usefulness of it. Beyond that, I'm still undecided. I'm keeping touch with people and places, so I'm not feeling any pressure to make a second decision. But I will, once this assignment is completed. I'm going to take time to pick something else I really will enjoy.

B: That's a nice surprise. Is there anything else?

E: When I review the topics covered in this book, I think of Donna's reaction in the prologue about needing to adjust slowly to the other side. You are probably correct in thinking the most radical thing is our sudden ability to see multiple lives which is not a common Earth concept. It might have been that concept that Donna found so unexpected.

Deceased folks usually come here expecting to be possessive of their individual families who they knew on Earth in their latest incarnation only to discover our definition of the family unit is dramatically wider. They have had many fathers, mothers, and siblings from different lives. Also, they may discover they have lingering prejudices to be worked on to reduce their impact later.

I hope this book project has broadened your view of the journey beyond death, Beverly, and has given you a heads up on what to expect when you arrive here.

B: Absolutely. Thanks.

❋ ❋ ❋

Spring 2019, Larry

Beverly (B), Larry (L)

B: How are you doing, Larry?

L: Okay, but I'm extremely busy. I'm officially out of the transitional period, so I'm having lots of conversations with friends and family from my Larry life. It's been quite a revelation and adjustment. You have no idea of the implications of how we affect each other and ourselves. Stunning is the only word I can use. [*chuckles*] It's like the Bette Davis' line, "Hang on; it's going to be a bumpy ride." It sure is a bumpy ride unlike any airplane I've ever been on! Anyway, it's all to the good, but in some cases it is hurtful.

But, I don't want to get sidetracked from your epilogue request I knew was coming.

B: Yes. What would you like to add for the reader?

L: Let me think. What would people find helpful? I heard you talking to Marv about conversing with people on different planes. Yes, what you did for me both while I was alive and then in transition over here, I found very helpful. You were "working both sides of the fence" when I was alive and when I moved over here. All that was good.

After the transition, it's important that people know everything is tailored to them—no generic sessions or classes. Everything is specific to you and your experiences. It is geared toward helping you get rid of anything that might hinder you in the future as you progress to the various levels. That's the marvelous part about how things are arranged here. So when working, I never feel like I'm doing busy work. It's all related to me and my history.

I think that's going to be more pronounced as time goes on. Lives accumulate a burden that we carry unless we can figure out how we are going to get rid of the baggage. With progress I'm permitted to go back and look at other lives, so I'll see how one life has affected the other. No matter who I am, what I've done both positive and negative, all this can be helped, so I can, in a sense, wash myself clean of any flaws that have become part of my nature through either lack of knowledge, carelessness, or any other reason. They are eager to help you lighten your load to have a happier, more productive life no matter where you are.

I find it quite marvelous how organized and helpful people here are; and I feel I'm in good hands from start to finish. I thank Elaine, you, and all the people who've given me support with their patience over the years. So, I am very happy with this whole process; and I feel optimistic.

I do understand now, Beverly, your anger at the Spreading of Ashes service.

B: [*deep sigh*] I apologize, Larry. It was over the top, but I guess it's comforting to both of us that it happened.

L: This is what you experienced in relationship with me, but now let's figure out how do we get rid of it. It's all a process for both of us. I'm happy that things seem to be going well for you; and I want that to continue. I know Elaine is thrilled with your progress. I wish you success with the book and its speedy publication. I'm sure there are other things you want to do.

B: Thank you, Larry, for your words of encouragement. Folks who fear a wrathful judgment, I hope, will be relieved to read your words.

❋ ❋ ❋

Spring 2019, Beverly

Each of my friends has taught me. To thank them I want to mention two of my favorite realizations they each have brought me during this book writing process:

From Nancy:

Just by thinking of a deceased person that brings my friend forth to me. What wonderful news to know it is not tough to stay connected with deceased friends. We are not separated even though I may not see them. We remain only a thought away.

Belief bubbles are nature's way of helping us get rid of our grief. I have felt those bubbles rising from my shoulders. Now I know they are real and serve a healing function in my body. I'm happy to know they are helping me release the pain of grief rather than forcing me to store that trauma.

From Joshua and Suzanne:

Josh, Suzanne, and I are soul fragments who have the same spirit guide with the goal of helping our soul group gain maturity. I've been lucky to discover and meet some of my soul fragments in this life and I'm overjoyed to know I'm part of a team. None of us are ever stranded alone.

Concentrating on my own worries, and fretting only about myself, can block out my ability to spot and assist others to find answers to their problems. This feeling of togetherness is also a part of knowing that I'm a member of a soul group team. Actually, all of us are equally important. The challenge is for all of us to consciously know and appreciate each other.

From Marvin:

Unless my self-image begins to change, I will end up in the same place I began at the beginning of this life. Thus, this life will not be as spiritually productive as I want. Either deal with problems here or on the other side. Storing unfinished business does not get rid of the issues. Missteps don't evaporate on their own. I've got to work at changing the inappropriate aspects of myself.

In order to work with past lives, I must unravel my situations in an orderly manner as suggested in the exercises so the previous lives have elbow room to delve into the details of their life—thus seeing connections between the lives. Again this sounds hard, but I'm happy to know others have successfully followed this path and reached their goal. If they can, so can I.

From Elaine:

My walk with Elaine through Eastcastle before her memorial service changed my life forever. Her demonstration of how it feels to lose something forever will always stick with me. Except for she and I, everything within eyeshot was an illusion. Only she and I were real, the rest were props on a stage. Being an art teacher and art historian, beauty was high on my priorities. You can imagine my shock at the sudden removal of all visual artifacts. What was important? What remained? Only we sisters. All else was secondary, temporary, dispensable.

Listening to the conversations of friends after Elaine's memorial, I understood the impact of seeing life only through my own veil. I am stunned. Varied views are colored by various circumstances, so seeing life from a mixture of people is important in the search for truth. Exposure to only my view is too limited.

From Larry:

The conscious me can telepathically talk to my unconscious friends and be heard at that level. Every little bit helps when trying to make contact. Nevertheless, I was shocked by the radical swings of feelings presented at the various levels of Larry's mind and grew to appreciate the torment that goes on in our heads. No wonder we are such volatile creatures.

What is stored in an unconscious mind is not necessarily part of their conscious awareness. Just because an idea is acknowledged, there is no guarantee the conscious person recognizes the information. So don't be surprised at denials or blank stares. We are complex organisms.

❊ ❊ ❊

To My Dear Friends, These Shining Stars,

I honor them, such brave, courageous souls who were willing to share their intimate and personal thoughts about their private challenges during some of the most vulnerable moments of their lives. Each of them is amazing to be willing to share those experiences with the reader and me to bring us new awareness. Life is a JOURNEY not a DESTINATION as we have been incorrectly taught. I humbly thank you.

Beverly

❊ ❊ ❊

Spring 2019 Samuel's message for Beverly:

B: [*kiddingly*] Well, Samuel, what was your part? What did you do?

S: Oh, Beverly, as always I helped once you saw you could assist. Remember, you, as the human, have to instigate matters! As I keep telling you, *You have to ask before I can respond.* I have all the answers—but you've got to ask the questions! I can't ask the questions. Even Marv gets it; he told you that one time from here—perfectly plain and simple.

Keep asking me questions, Beverly!

B: [*blushing*] Will do.

※ ※ ※

Spring 2019, Samuel's message for the readers:

Of all the people under my guardianship and tutelage, there are none more earnest than the three folks, Beverly, Joshua, and Suzanne, in their stories that you have read about in these pages. Each in their specific ways has talents and abilities that help them drive forward in their searches for understanding and perfection. I'm grateful for their dedication to searching for answers to life's problems as they have explained in these pages.

It is my wish that the readers apply the same sincerity they bring to the fore. It is only through diligently applied effort that you, too, will have the success they have achieved. It is possible to make great strides in one lifetime. Yes, you can achieve as much success.

I encourage you to call upon your own spirit guides today for assistance in your efforts to remove the stains and blemishes tarnishing your soul. You will find we spirit guides are eager to help you advance at whatever pace you set. Please don't put it off, no matter what phase of life you are in. It's the nicest thing you can do for yourself, bar none.

Samuel (as known to Beverly)

Author Biography

The wedding photo on the following page puts you back at one of my major, life-turning points as Dad and I prepare to walk down the chapel aisle to join Marvin, the groom. The casual observer would never have guessed the panicky thoughts pulsating in our brains—each expressing their own fears. Was this marriage a wise move? The best move? A required move?

Would I follow my life outline? This question hung in the balance during those next few moments. In those days I knew nothing about spiritual life plans called outlines. Had Marv and I not married, perhaps I might not have been introduced to the concept. For that matter, I probably wouldn't know about spirit guides, conversing with dead friends, or finding peace with my previous, yet intrusive, past lives such as that of a sorceress begging for attention.

Doing all those things has allowed me to delve into the transitional phase between life on Earth and life on the other side. Such a fascinating journey tells me *What Dead People Taught Me* needs to be my next book, a sequel to this one.

Beverly and father Ray walk to her wedding 1960
University of Wisconsin Graduate
Art Teacher
Church Secretary
Historic Drapery Reproductions
Author with Father

Glossary

Akashic Record: The energetic history of each individual soul who ever existed.

Astral travel: The ability of the non-physical body to move energetically to other locations.

Channeling: The ability to calm one's own mental and physical state and move into another's mental and physical state to pick up their words.

Chill: Validation that a message has been correctly understood by a human.

Clairaudience: Hearing what is thought to be inaudible.

Clairvoyance: Perceiving beyond regular five senses.

Connectors: Souls whose job is to help humans bond deeply with others.

Crossed spirit: A deceased person who has gone through the light and entered the other side of existence.

Dimensional Psychic: Communication between giver and receiver located on different planes of existence.

Empathic: A person acutely sensitive to the emotions of others.

Exit Points: Planned moments in an outline where a person can permanently opt to leave their body.

Grounders: Spirits who help encourage stability and balance in living souls.

Ghosts: Deceased humans who have not crossed over to the other side are to continue healing their unresolved issues from a new perspective close to Earth.

Heaven: Popularly considered to be the ultimate location to be with God.

Hell: Large and small illusionary pockets of self-styled misery to contain people who decide to punish themselves after death.

Hell-work: The rescue by souls of deceased humans who have imprisoned themselves in their own hell.

Home: The plane where spirits live between lifetimes. Earthlings call it the other side.

Invisible Structure: An organized, multifaceted format for the evolution of one's soul to point them back to Source.

Knowing: The psychic ability of spontaneously fully understanding a concept without having to piece together the parts.

Life Theme: A predetermined topic (rejection, abandonment, etc.) a soul chooses to have while moving through life on Earth. Everything a soul experiences is filtered through its screen.

Light: A light created after death to transport soul from one level to another.

Medium: A psychic with the ability to channel dead people.

Normie: A person not aware of the spiritual side of their existence.

Outline: A segment of a detailed energy plan of how our soul will travel through the multi-level, invisible structure to bring us back to our God-self. A person's specific decision is made in the flesh.

Obsession: A ghost invades a person's aura looking for safety and influence on a human.

Possession: A ghost invades the physical body of another human to seek control and life.

Prayer: The universe's savings and loan bank of spiritual energy.

Protection: Shield for humans to repel unwanted energies invading their space.

Residue: Lingering emotional energy imprinted after an intense event.

Rejuvenators: Spirits who help return the deceased to the person they were before they died.

Sensitive: Intuitive people who are aware when they are in the presence of unseen emotions.

Soothers: Spirits who attend to the comfort of those newly rescued from their hell.

Soul cluster: Spirits who share the same occupational mission.

Soul fragments: Individual segments of the same soul that has divided.

Soulmates: Fragments of the first generation of the same soul (similar to twins)

Source: God

Spirit guides: Specific spirits with human experience assigned as a journey companion and advisor.

The other side: The pre and post-Earth location for spirits. Also called home.

Warriors: Souls who volunteer to help rescue the deceased living in hell.

Intertwined Souls Over Lifetimes

Bev's Beliefs & Baggage	Beverly's Era		Sorceress' Era	
	Name	Role	Role	Result
Insecure, Guilt, Anger, Detachment from Children	Beverly	Author	Sorceress	Suicide and individual hell
Motherly, Disappointed, Rejected	Marvin	Husband of Author	Toddler Son	Poisoned by Mother's Foe
Loyal, Proud, Protective, Guilt	Elaine	Sister of Author	Elder Daughter of Sorceress	Killed by Sorceress
Guilt, Concern, Responsible	Mary*	Maternal Great-grandmother	Youngest Daughter	Killed by Sorceress
Fearful, Distrust, Hurt	Larry	Brother-in-law of Author	Foe of Sorceress	Ordered poisoning of Sorceress' Toddler

Please note: the beliefs and baggage traits repeat themselves in both eras of the same reincarnated person.

* Few details of Mary's life have been revealed, either through genealogy or psychically.

www.ingramcontent.com/pod-product-compliance
Lightning Source LLC
Chambersburg PA
CBHW030051100526
44591CB00008B/108